Twayne's United States Authors Series

Sylvia E. Bowman, *Editor*

INDIANA UNIVERSITY

William Saroyan

WILLIAM SAROYAN

By HOWARD R. FLOAN
Manhattan College

Twayne Publishers, Inc. :: New York

Library of Congress Catalog Card Number: 66-12051

MANUFACTURED IN THE UNITED STATES OF AMERICA BY
UNITED PRINTING SERVICES, INC.
NEW HAVEN, CONNECTICUT

To
my brother
Len

Preface

THE WRITINGS of William Saroyan fall into four periods distinct in genre and varied in tone. The first of these, a period of short fiction, begins in 1934 with *The Daring Young Man on the Flying Trapeze* and culminates in the stories of *My Name is Aram,* most of which were written by 1939. The second, a period of drama, extends from 1939, the year of *My Heart's in the Highlands* and *The Time of Your Life,* to 1943, when he turned his attention once more to prose fiction. During these years all of his well-known plays, with the exception of *The Cave Dwellers,* appeared on Broadway. The third, a period characterized by the novel, begins with *The Human Comedy* (1943) and ends in 1953 with *The Laughing Matter,* the last of a series which moves toward increasingly tragic effects. Since *The Laughing Matter,* his work has been much more casual in purpose and miscellaneous in scope. Though this fourth period is characterized by a variety of literary kinds, it is distinguished from its predecessors by the addition of autobiography. Since *The Bicycle Rider in Beverly Hills* (1952), he has written two other autobiographical interludes, *Here Comes / There Goes / You Know Who* (1961) and *Not Dying* (1963).

During the first two of these periods, Saroyan won wide popular acclaim and the support of some of our finest critics—and this writing continues to interest us most. I have therefore devoted the most detailed attention to this early work, tracing the young Saroyan's search for the right subject and for a technique suitable to it. I have also examined carefully his efforts to adapt his narrative techniques to the novel. Saroyan's writings have continued to appear in unabashed abundance, often eliciting wry comments to the effect that he performs "with the greatest of ease." Though much of this criticism is justifiable, it must be recognized that Saroyan, like the trapeze artist, worked hard to make his work look easy—and always like fun. The surest sign of his professional competence has been his ability to retain this air of unrehearsed spontaneity while concentrating on problems of his craft.

Over the years his voice has been inimitable and consistently authentic. At his best he has spoken to us meaningfully of things hitherto unexpressed in our literature. His writing therefore deserves serious critical attention. Until now it has been the subject of very few articles beyond the initial reviews, and there has been no book-length study. In this book I have tried to assess the strength and weakness of his work. I have also sought to define the unique quality of his imagination, to account for his enormous popular appeal and for the obvious staying power of this appeal. I have kept my eye directly on his texts and have turned to the literary and social environment only to gain necessary perspectives on the nature of his work and the responses which it has evoked.

HOWARD R. FLOAN

Bronxville, New York
April, 1965

Acknowledgments

For permission to quote from material under copyright I wish to thank Mr. William Saroyan and the following publishers: Harcourt, Brace and World, Putnam's, Random House, and Little, Brown and Company. Portions of Chapter Four appeared originally in *Thought*, XXXIII (Spring, 1958), under the title, "Saroyan and Cervantes' Knight," and also in *Atlántico* (1959) in Spanish translation.

I wish to express my gratitude to the following persons who have contributed importantly to the writing of this book: to Professor Sylvia E. Bowman, for suggesting that I undertake this study and for her highly competent editorial direction; to Brother Celestine Eugene, Dr. Paul Cortissoz, and Dr. Howard Warger, of the Manhattan College Department of English, for their perceptive critical reading of large portions of the manuscript; to Mrs. Dorothea Mestice, for preparing the typescript; and to my wife Maxine for her constant understanding and for her keen and responsive reading of the manuscript in its various phases of completion.

Contents

Chronology

1908 William Saroyan born in Fresno, California, the fourth child of Armenak and Takoohi Saroyan.

1911 Father died. William, his brother Henry, and his sisters, Cosette and Zabel, placed in an orphanage in Oakland. In order to visit the children on weekends their mother took a job in nearby San Francisco.

1915 Family returned to Fresno where William attended public schools. At the age of eight he began selling papers for the *Fresno Evening Herald.* Over the years he had miscellaneous after-school jobs, especially that of telegraph messenger boy. Left high school before graduation.

1926 In San Francisco, worked at various jobs. Became clerk and then telegraph operator for Postal Telegraph Company.

1927 Manager of branch office of Postal Telegraph Company.

1928 Published story in *Overland Monthly and Outwest Magazine.* Decided to make writing his career. First trip to New York.

1933 Published story in *Hairenik,* Armenian journal.

1934 Published his first book, *The Daring Young Man on the Flying Trapeze.*

1935 Second trip to New York.

1936 Published *Inhale and Exhale* and *Three Times Three.* Employed as writer on weekly salary by B. P. Schulberg in Hollywood.

1937 Published *Little Children.*

1938 Published *Love, Here is My Hat* and *The Trouble with Tigers.*

1939 *My Heart's in the Highlands* opened on Broadway in April; *The Time of Your Life* in October. The latter he wrote in six days at the Great Northern Hotel, New York. In the summer, traveled to London, Dublin, and Paris.

1940 In January, his ballet-play, "A Theme in the Life of the Great American Goof," opened in New York. Received Pulitzer Prize and New York Drama Critics' Circle Award for best play of 1939-1940 season, *The Time of Your Life.* He rejected the Pulitzer Prize. *Love's Old Sweet Song* opened on Broadway in April. Published *My Name is Aram.*

1941 In April, directed and produced on Broadway his own play, *The Beautiful People.* In December, went to Metro-Goldwyn-Mayer in Hollywood to write a scenario, "The Human Comedy," and to direct a short movie of his own composition.

1942 In August, directed and produced on Broadway two of his own plays: *Across the Board on Tomorrow Morning* and *Talking to You.* Sworn into army in October. *Hello Out There* opened on Broadway in September.

1943 In February, married Carol Marcus in Ohio, where he was stationed as a Private in the Signal Corps. Published *The Human Comedy. Get Away Old Man* opened on Broadway in November. Birth of his son Aram.

1944 Served with Signal Corps in London. Published *Dear Baby.* Wrote *The Adventures of Wesley Jackson.*

1945 Discharged from the army at Fort Lewis, Washington, in September, after thirteen months overseas duty.

1946 Birth of daughter Lucy.

1947 Published a play, *Jim Dandy: Fat Man in a Famine.* Brought his family to New York, where he leased a house near Oyster Bay, Long Island.

1949 Published several plays: *Don't Go Away Mad; Sam Ego's House; A Decent Birth, A Happy Funeral.* Divorced from Carol Marcus in Reno.

1950 Published *The Assyrian and Other Stories* and *Twin Adventures.*

1951 Published *Rock Wagram* and *Tracy's Tiger*. His song, "Come On-a My House," a hit in America and abroad. Second marriage to Carol Marcus.

1952 Published the first of his book-length autobiographical sketches, *The Bicycle Rider in Beverly Hills*. Divorced from Carol Marcus in Santa Monica, California.

1953 Published *The Laughing Matter*.

1956 Published *The Whole Voyald and Other Stories* and *Mama I Love You*.

1957 *The Cave Dwellers* opened on Broadway in October. Published *Papa You're Crazy*.

1958 Gave up his home at Malibu Beach, California, where he had lived for six years and began extensive travel abroad. He continues to spend much time abroad, making his principal home in Paris. In October, a television adaptation of *The Time of Your Life* with Jackie Gleason was produced on "Playhouse 90."

1959 *Ah Sweet Mystery of Mrs. Murphy* produced by NBC Television. Saroyan in Yugoslavia with tentative plans to make a movie.

1960 *The Paris Comedy, or the Secret of Lily* opened in Vienna. *The London Comedy, or Sam the Highest Jumper of them All* opened in London, as did *Settled Out of Court*, which he wrote with Henry Cecil.

1961 Writer in residence at Purdue University. *High Time Along the Wabash* produced at the University Playhouse.

1962 *The Unstoppable Gray Fox* produced on CBS Television.

1963 Published *Boys and Girls Together*.

1964 Published *One Day in the Afternoon of the World*.

William Saroyan

CHAPTER *1*

The Daring Young Man

WHEN WHIT BURNETT and Martha Foley accepted "The Daring Young Man on the Flying Trapeze" for the February, 1934, issue of *Story*, they soon began to believe that in its author, William Saroyan, they had discovered the most significant literary talent to appear in San Francisco since Jack London and Frank Norris.[1] They had never known a more instantaneous, enthusiastic response to a new contributor. Here was the literature of protest that was in fashion, but its manner and spirit were new and different. The title itself offered a welcome dash of ironic spice, and its protagonist appealed in a very special way to the intellectuals of the day, both on and off the campus, because he combined the esthete's responsiveness to life with the stoic's resignation to the death which he chose in preference to a mindless pursuit of survival in an insensitive, industrialized world.

In April the editors of *Story* published "Seventy Thousand Assyrians," a better story than its predecessor; and in May "The Shepherd's Daughter," an Oriental fable which Saroyan recounts with fitting simplicity but concludes with a whimsical wink to his reader. In this issue the editors noted that William Saroyan was by now well known to *Story* readers. "If the reception of his first story," they said, "brought him dozens of letters of appreciation from other writers, 'Seventy Thousand Assyrians' last month won him a general public."[2] In this same month *American Mercury* published "Aspirin is a Member of the N.R.A." and added another Saroyan piece in August. Soon *Scribner's, The Yale Review, The New Republic, Scholastic, Harper's, The Atlantic Monthly,* and others included him in their lists of contributors. By October, 1934, Random House was able to assemble twenty-six stories and a preface for Saroyan's first book, *The Daring Young Man on the Flying Trapeze.*[3] Though many were troubled by the obvious unevenness of this collection, its freshness and originality were everywhere acknowledged. In less than one year from his first appearance in *Story*, William Saroyan had become one of the most widely discussed writers of the time.

To appreciate the impact of Saroyan's first volume when it appeared some thirty years ago is difficult for one who reads it today, for he must re-create the mood of the depression era in order to understand its sense of the freshness of this new writer. Saroyan's urge to write was a spontaneous assertion of his ebullient sense of being alive, which for him was less awareness of self than responsiveness to life about him. What gives vitality to the projected personality is its involvement in a concrete, believable setting. In looking back to Saroyan's sudden and spectacular appearance on the literary scene, it seems incontestable that a large part of the enthusiasm for his work consisted of a fascination for the spirit of the times, for what it meant in human terms to live through the grim economic crisis of the Great Depression. In nine of its pieces, approximately one-third of the book, the daring young man is a writer, and in only three of these is he presented as supposedly other than Saroyan himself. But in none of the stories did Saroyan get very far in trying to project an imagined character different from himself. About his first book he might have said, echoing Montaigne, "I am myself the substance of my book . . . It is myself that I portray." But unlike Montaigne, or those who have followed the urbane Frenchman in writing the personal essay, Saroyan was not making an *enquiry* into himself or measuring his response to ideas. Paradoxically, he was autobiographical without being especially aware of himself or of his own processes of thought.

I The Daring Young Man on the Flying Trapeze

His first book aroused more conjecture than judgment. The Preface itself, instead of offering the usual clarifications, presented a series of comments astonishingly flippant and ambiguous.[4] It began facetiously with the author's promise that, if the book proved successful, he would supply a continuing and life-long series of prefaces for all future editions; and it expressed the hope that, after his death, there would be children and grandchildren to carry on the good work. With equal jauntiness he informed his readers that in grammar school he had discovered the falseness of rules governing fictions and that he would disregard Edgar Allan Poe, O. Henry, and all others. One must forget that one is a writer, he said, and simply put words together the best that one can. His rule would be to ignore all rules—and learn to typewrite so that he could turn out stories as fast as Zane Grey.

Despite this impudence, however, those who kept the book's title in mind would have been inclined not to accept the professed naïveté and anti-intellectualism of the Preface at face value, but to consider it as the tongue-in-cheek remarks of a young sophisticate who understood the current reaction against the well-educated, highly literate writers of the "genteel tradition." Such a declaration of independence, no matter how forward, seemed to many not only appropriate but promising in a young writer. Perhaps this was his zany way of expressing a determination to look into his heart and write and to learn to write by writing, not altogether unusual applications of American self-reliance. And Saroyan's effort to see the writer as a man speaking to men helped justify the attitude running through his fiction that he wished to give his readers not art but life itself—an assertion which to us at mid-century may seem to deny art its rightful due, but which pleased the earlier preference for talented amateurism.

Up to this point, at least, the reader of that day could choose his interpretation of the Preface: it was a sophomoric defiance of all tutors, or a salutary proclamation of freedom from stylistic traditions. If he associated the remarks of the Preface with the stories that followed, however, the perceptive reader may well have feared that this avowedly preface-minded newcomer would turn out to be not a short-story writer at all but an overly self-conscious essayist whose entire work would consist of a series of prefaces thinly disguised as fiction.

But the flippancy and ambiguity vanish in the closing passages in which Saroyan speaks of the distinguishing marks of the earnest writer. Brief though they are, these comments help to identify what I believe is a distinctive aspect of the authentic voice of Saroyan: his constant awareness that life is lived in the presence of death. Born and reared among the Armenians of the San Joaquin Valley, emigrants from a country that had many times faced extinction and had known almost endless hardships, Saroyan soon learned the harsh conditions under which life was often given to man. Suffering and death were unalterable facts to which one had to become reconciled. To Saroyan the inevitability of death implied, despite all feeling to the contrary, that it was as natural as birth and therefore not *in itself* a matter of tragedy. Indeed, its very closeness heightened for him the sense of preciousness of one's moment of life. That which man feared most was paradoxically the source of his dignity, and even of his humor: "If you will remember that living people are as good as dead, you will be able to perceive much that is very funny in their conduct that you perhaps might never have thought of perceiving if you did not believe that they were as good as dead."

Saroyan's sense of irony, one of the identifying marks of his early fiction, was compounded of this awareness of death and of an intensified responsiveness to life. It made possible the incongruous but enormously effective metaphor of his title, and it imparted an indefinable charm to this first book. The Preface closes with the assertion that one must learn to breathe deeply, to taste, and even to sleep with as much zest and responsiveness as one's capacities permit: "Try to be alive. You will be dead soon enough." For those who knew the privations of the depression, this plea to make the most of life's simple joys struck a responsive note, and they welcomed this new writer as one who seemed to possess a poet's instinct to express what they themselves had come to feel.

It was to this mood that the title story, "The Daring Young Man on the Flying Trapeze," especially addressed itself, evoking an emotional response that exceeded in its intensity any rationally conceived evaluation of the story itself.[5] It is an interior monologue in which fragments of thought and impressions, derived from reading and personal experience, pass through the mind of a young writer who is dying of starvation. These recollections, mostly involuntary in nature, reveal the sensitive mind of the youth while at the same time they suggest the myriad and rich possibilities of human experience. This contrast between promise and denial generates the emotional force of the story. In 1934 it seemed particularly timely to those who felt ironic about the disparity between America's great productive power and the privations suffered because of her economic ills. Moreover, the range of the young man's associations extended to the growing unrest abroad, for thoughts of Stalin and Hitler and "a multitude of Jews" flashed through his mind. What seemed to be in jeopardy was not only this young writer but also the very lifeblood of civilization, for in himself he suggested something of the bewilderment and discouragement felt by intellectuals everywhere.

Yet the youth in the story achieved an aloofness from the troublesome present, too, because his inner world reached back to Jerusalem and Rome, included Shakespeare and Eliot, Dostoevsky and Flaubert, jazz and "Finlandia," and mathematics "highly polished and slick as a green onion to the teeth." In his short life he lived for ages and had known many things, both good and evil. Only a part of him, a superficial part, needed to go through the weary, hopeless motions of once again seeking employment; and this side of his being he regarded with amused tolerance. As he shaved and put on his only necktie, he grinned at his reflection in the mirror and noted that he was very unhandsome. Leaving his small room and walking along the streets of San Francisco, he admired the majesty of the city, but he felt outside of it and was certain that he would never gain admittance. Perhaps he had "ventured upon the wrong earth or into the wrong age."

The black coffee and cigarettes which had been his only sustenance for days seemed to induce a clarified flow of images: his visions of food had the beauty of a still-life, and what he regretted most about his approaching death was that there would not be time to read again *Hamlet* or *Huck Finn.* But in his weakened state he had little control over the conscious processes of thought, and his mind played tricks on him. He was amused by the ironic appropriateness of the popular song that kept running through his mind: "He flies through the air with the greatest of ease, the daring young man on the flying trapeze." It was "astoundingly funny," he thought, "a trapeze to God, or to nothing, a flying trapeze to some sort of eternity."

On the conscious levels of his mind the youth was serene and unperturbed. At times, however, bitterness welled up within him, as when he thought of the conceited, slovenly clerk at the employment office—perhaps the only human being whom he could regard as a representative of the vast, impersonal system. The youth was angered by the thought that to buy food he had sold his books—nine of them for eighty-five cents. But, more characteristically, his resentment expressed itself in ironic actions: He stole a dozen sheets of letter paper from the Y.M.C.A. on which he planned to write "An Application for Permission to Live," and he polished with great care a copper penny which he found in the gutter, reading with thoughtful deliberation the words: "E Pluribus Unum One Cent United States of America . . . In God We Trust Liberty 1923."

Returning to his room in the afternoon, he met one of the swiftest, most painless and fearless deaths in all modern literature. Saroyan had said in the Preface that one need not portray death as "dramatically tragic," and the romantic sentiment that permeated this story was attenuated considerably by his avoidance of the tragic. Nevertheless, he added voltage to this death scene by tapping into several reliable sources of sentiment. His young man lost nothing by death because "for an eternal moment he was all things at once: the bird, the fish, the rodent, the reptile, and man." Furthermore, there was the instinctive pleasure of vengeance, for at his death the world, not he, was judged: "The city burned. The herded crowd rioted." And beyond this tumult one experienced a liberating, cosmic vision as "the earth circled away," and the youth "turned his lost face to the empty sky and became dreamless, unalive, perfect." It was a death that assuaged the reader's fears without committing him to logic or religious orthodoxy: the young man's spirit, though unalive in an empty sky, was somehow perfect. But the sky was not really empty, for one felt that the entire scene was enacted before an assembly of great universal spirits like Shakespeare and Dostoevsky who witnessed the young man's martyrdom and who lent dignity and consolation to an otherwise pathetic, meaningless incident.

"The Daring Young Man" deserved much of the enthusiasm which it aroused. Its mood, not of contempt for material things, but a sense of their triviality, conveys a stoical aloofness without diminishing one's feeling for the preciousness of "the swift moment of life." Its style, discursive and impressionistic, is appropriate to the nature of the dying man's thoughts. In keeping with the note of objectivity suggested by the title, Saroyan used the third-person narrative technique, but retained the immediacy of the first-person by assuming complete and intimate knowledge of the mind of his character. Thus the outward action of the story, slight as it is, establishes a structural unity while remaining subordinated to the inner life of his character. Because the life surrounding the youth is seen only as it impinges upon his consciousness, the story achieves an effect not unlike that of an impressionistic painting of Edouard Manet or of Pierre Renoir.

Saroyan's personal identification with the writer in his story was so thorough and pervasive that, with little apparent effort, he was able to suffuse the work with all the emotions that had built up within him during his first difficult years in San Francisco. This oneness with his character, however, despite the force it imparted to the story, proved to be the source of its greatest blemish. Although Saroyan assured his reader that the young man knew no self-pity, one finds it hard to exonerate Saroyan himself from this charge. The tears are held in check, but the story has an unmistakable hear-this-and-weep tone. Thus it is motivated, at least in part, by an extra-literary plea for sympathy and support for underprivileged authors.

II *Beyond the Title Story*

The dangers of Saroyan's autobiographical impulse are more clearly revealed in another story of this volume, "Aspirin is a Member of the N.R.A." Similar to "The Daring Young Man" in subject and conception but different in technique, it fails, despite the excellence of its essential idea, because its narrative form, that of recollected experience told in the first person, held temptations for Saroyan which he was then unable to withstand. As in "The Daring Young Man," the tragedy implicit in the alienation of the young artist in this story must derive ironic force from the fact that he does not see himself as tragic, or even as pathetic. Its effectiveness depends upon a double vision: the author must provide his reader with a view which includes but exceeds what he allows to his narrator. Because Saroyan fails to keep himself apart from his fictional speaker, however, he cannot sustain this double vision; and the possibilities of his original conception, essentially dramatic in nature, are never realized. If the opening lines could be regarded as the words of a confused young man sitting alone in the darkness of a small room, smoking cigarettes and waiting for morning, their awkward pretentiousness would be acceptable as presumably appropriate to the emotional state of an imagined character; but, because the speaker never achieves distinct fictional identity, one must read his words as Saroyan's own musings. Moreover, spoken after the event, they nevertheless lack the restraint and clarity of retrospect. This failure to accept the discipline necessary to his chosen form prevents the story from coming into focus, and it makes especially objectionable the careless use of fragmented impressions throughout the story, as well as the two or three passages that come out like ill-digested Hemingway.[6] In comparing these two stories, one realizes how right Saroyan was to kill off his daring young man, even though it was perhaps a desperate way to preserve the distinction between author and character.

How closely these two stories were written out of Saroyan's own personal experience is shown by "A Cold Day," which makes no attempt to cast into fictional form an account of his efforts to write under similar conditions of hardship. Published originally in *Story* (April, 1934) as a letter to Martha Foley, it was included with only a change of title in this first volume. Although rather trying because of Saroyan's assumption that it should present every whimsy of his mind, the sketch nevertheless achieves a tone of spontaneity and ease and communicates a feeling of intimacy and involvement that is essential to this kind of writing. It acquires also a certain charm from Saroyan's knack of laughing at himself even as he indulges in self-pity and asks, too, for a little of his reader's admiration.

There are other pieces about the young author which present Saroyan directly without projecting into any fictional form either author or theme. "Common Prayer" is an impressionistic and disorderly thanksgiving for an acceptance slip. "Three Stories," an inchoate essay notwithstanding its title, expresses on the one hand Saroyan's disdain for people who attend formal concerts for social rather than artistic reasons, and on the other hand his wish to get simple, authentic life into his prose. "Myself Upon the Earth" and "A Shepherd's Daughter," which will be discussed later, are in this vein.

On the other hand, one meets in his pages such people as John Melovich, Pat Ferrara, a student named Paul, and other variations of Saroyan's ubiquitous "I," but rarely do they achieve individuality in their own right. He tended to insinuate himself into these stories without providing a place for himself. Yet the irrepressibility of his personality, though conflicting with the basic design of the characters, contributes what is most valuable to them and makes them interesting even as failures. The story of John Melovich, for example, gains enormously by an impressionistic flash-back to a past that differs in no essential way from that of Saroyan himself. Despite its impossible title, "The Earth, Day, Night, Self" is the best of the stories which attempt to create a character distinct from the author.[7]

Those that present a better adjustment of subject and narrative technique are "And Man" and "Fight Your Own War." The first of these uses the form of recalled experience told in the first person to make plausible and moving an emotional crisis of an awkward teen-ager. The second tells of an Italian-American writer in San Francisco who struggles tenaciously to stick to his writing despite poverty and the menace of approaching war. Although we may never think of Enrico Sturiza as anybody other than Saroyan himself, this story loses nothing thereby; for, by adapting his own personality to a slightly fictionalized circumstance, Saroyan imparted warmth and vitality to his protagonist, visualized his setting effectively, and conveyed through a believable conflict the tragi-comic aspect of a rather eccentric artist out of tune with his times. If after thirty years the story has come to seem somewhat quaint, I think it is because world events have made too obvious for credibility the naïveté of the protagonist's exasperated exclamation: "Why don't they fight their own war?" But the story shows clearly that Saroyan had a talent for direct, straightforward narrative.[8]

The same competence is notable in "Harry," which tells of "a real American go-getter" who could sell anything to anybody. Having burned himself out in a brief but vigorous life, he remains the entrepreneur even on his deathbed: he occupies his thoughts with schemes for selling life-insurance. Through the effective use of a narrator, Saroyan catches the right tone, for the speaker is naïvely receptive to the American success story, especially to the more sensational versions; and his awed admiration for Harry cannot be stifled by thoughts of trickery and the social and moral cost of his opportunism. But he has a sense of humor, too, and perceives the community's need for colorful people. Through his eyes, a small town takes on life. Yet he does not realize how much he tells about himself and his society, for Saroyan provides the reader with a broader point of view than that of his speaker. The result is satirical humor that turns back upon the narrator but at the same time questions implicitly the values of the whole community.

But at heart Saroyan was neither rebel nor satirist, and thus "Fight Your Own War" and "Harry," though competently written, do not reflect the most distinctive marks of his imagination. The real promise of this first book lay in the author's instinct for a kind of writing so intimately bound up with his own life that he could develop it, not by withholding, but by adapting and shaping his own personality. His most successful attempt in this respect is "Seventy Thousand Assyrians," in which he installs himself as narrator in order to gain the immediacy and credibility of his presence and yet he overcomes the usual limiting effects of autobiographical devices by telling of those whose backgrounds differ widely from his own.

In this story the author has left his writing desk and walked to the barber school on Third Avenue in San Francisco to get a fifteen-cent haircut—the only kind he can afford. In the shop he talks with a boy from Iowa who is roaming the country in search of work; he watches a young Japanese apprentice shave a tramp in the free chair and try pathetically to avoid the old fellow's breath; he thinks of the Japanese with whom he had worked in the vineyards of the San Joaquin Valley and tries to recall their difficult names. His own barber, an Assyrian named Theodore Badal, tells of his vanishing race: "There are only seventy thousand Assyrians left in the world," he said, "and the Arabs are still killing us. They killed seventy of us in a little uprising last month. There was a small paragraph in the paper. Seventy more of us destroyed. We'll be wiped out before long. My brother is married to an American girl and he has a son. . . . We are trying to forget Assyria. My father still reads a paper that comes from New York, but he is an old man. He will be dead soon."[9]

The various elements of the story all come together in the responsiveness of the narrator, who perceives that dignity has less to do with dress and buying power than with composure in the face of privation and loss. The tone of the piece is precisely suited to its setting. Saroyan is not writing a story, he insists, but is simply chatting informally—and in a facetious, slightly embarrassed manner—about a supposedly trivial occurrence in his own life. Yet he sees with the artist's observant eye, with the penetration of one who understands the poverty of the men in the shop, and with the craftsman's instinctive habit of speculating about how to get the experience into a story. This last characteristic is particularly notable; for, in sharing the casual conjectures of this narrator, the reader finds himself caught up actively and intimately in the process of transforming life into art. This seemingly amorphous recollection, while professing to do very little indeed, turns out to be a highly serious presentation of the dismay and insecurity that dwell just beneath the placid externals of daily life. Deeply meaningful in a day of economic unrest at home and of political upheavals abroad, this story was well received when it first appeared; and it has not lost its effectiveness with the years. Though overshadowed by "The Daring Young Man," it says more—and says it with stronger originality.

III *Literary Influences*

The narrator of "Seventy Thousand Assyrians" remarks that readers of Sherwood Anderson will understand what he is saying and will know that his laughter is sad. The story reminds one of

Anderson, but not so much in content and quality of laughter as in its establishing as unifying intelligence a young writer who is really the author himself, and in its method of illuminating the inner life of a character by a sudden evocation of an image. Yet Saroyan was more himself in "Seventy Thousand Assyrians" than in stories like the oddly named "1,2,3,4,5,6,7,8" which turn on the loneliness of the individual and his inability to communicate his most private thoughts, stories which owe much to Anderson.

This odd title refers to a passage of syncopation in a jazz piece which is played repeatedly on a phonograph by a nineteen-year-old boy who lives alone in a three-dollar-a-week room. It is a break in the rhythmical pattern which takes on peculiar significance for the boy who is in desperate need of individual expression. He has a brief and uneventful affair with a lonely young woman whose life, like his own, is dominated by the impersonal machines of the teletype room where both are employed. Amid all this elaborate equipment for communications they live in almost complete personal isolation. No specific reason is given for the break-up of the brief romance, for the story underlines the mystery of human aloneness. But the final impression is not of mystery but of recognition: the pathos of the young man is that he wants more from life than he thinks it can give. The story has great potential and invites comparison with Anderson, but at the same time one notes Saroyan's uncertainty in devising his own technique. Despite promising experiments with symbolic effects, the narrative fails because of Saroyan's ill-advised attempt to use both the first- and third-person point of view, presumably hoping with the one to enter more believably into the intimate thoughts of his character without foregoing the more objective view that is possible to the other. This repeated shifting becomes a mannerism which draws attention to itself and, as it is an obvious flaw, shows a regrettable unwillingness on the part of Saroyan to rework his material.

Although Saroyan's first book belongs to San Francisco, the presence of Fresno is strongly felt. Like Anderson looking back to his small Ohio village, Saroyan had absorbed the earlier experience of his life more deeply and more thoroughly. His knowledge of the struggling immigrants of the San Joaquin Valley enabled him to see beneath the impersonal surfaces of the cosmopolitan city. Reading Anderson no doubt helped him recognize the availability of his home town and the value of using himself and his family as a center of reference. It was probably from Anderson, too, that he learned to reveal the true nature of an individual's life, not through a developed sequence of events—Saroyan rarely gives us narrative in this linear sense—but by means of a sudden flash of recognition that comes through symbolic gesture, a dramatized moment in time that implies an entire life.

Saroyan no doubt recognized his kinship with Anderson. Much of his fiction constitutes a sort of "Story-Teller's Story" and is similar to Anderson in many ways: its indifference to plot; its underplaying of technique and overplaying of spontaneity and sincerity; its tendency to indulge in homely philosophy; its preference for eccentrics and outcasts; its delicacy in handling sex, relating it more to loneliness than to passion; its scorn for what Anderson called "dreary commercial success"; its contempt for formal education; its distrust of churches and religious creeds combined with a strong religiosity and an almost mystical reverence and humility before the possibilities of life.

Later, in discussing *Inhale and Exhale,* more will be said about Saroyan's struggle to assimilate what he learned from Anderson. But Saroyan is an unlikely subject for the exploration of literary influences. Always defiantly unliterary, he has repeatedly expressed contempt for rules and stylistic traditions. Although he spent much time in the public libraries of Fresno and San Francisco, his reading was fragmentary and cursory. "Big Valley Vineyard" expresses his desire as a writer to augment and clarify his direct personal experience with knowledge drawn from literature. But his attempts to draw upon his reading—or upon reading as an activity—for either subject or theme were not successful. "Big Valley Vineyard" is impossibly vague as an autobiographical sketch, it cannot be called fiction, and as an essay it fails through lack of inner coherence. "Among the Lost" is a conscious effort to make the two orders of experience mutually illuminating by telling of a young writer named Paul who reads English poetry amid the squalor of a San Francisco bar and gambling room. Though fragments of poems, especially of T. S. Eliot's "Prufrock," are interspersed throughout the young man's musings, the sketch turns out to be nothing more than literary name-dropping.

The Daring Young Man is remarkably original for a first book. Reviewers and critics, quick to place new writers in respect to fashions and categories, were notably silent on the subject of influences. One of the few exceptions was Burton Rascoe, who wrote: "He is original. I see no traceable influence except that of Sherwood Anderson, the untutored, homely honesty of whose early writings Mr. Saroyan has apparently absorbed."[10] And Edmund Wilson, speaking of stylistic fashions, remarked that Saroyan derived from Hemingway. There are times when *The Daring Young Man* sounds like Hemingway, but they are not many; and, as Edmund Wilson also noted, Saroyan was hardly to be classified with the hard-boiled writers.[11] Hemingway's influence was of course real, but even in this first book it was beneath the surface and consisted primarily of the ideals of sparseness and of trust in the uses of concrete details. But Saroyan would not be fully ready to embody these ideals until his third book.

Yet *The Daring Young Man* has many signs of those afternoons spent in the public reading rooms. To note some of them now indicates something about the sensibilities and aims of Saroyan when he first began to publish and about the literary climate of that time. The influence of Walt Whitman seems to have escaped readers of 1934—at least it goes unremarked in the reviews. Perhaps Whitman was too much a part of that day for his influence to be regarded as noteworthy. Yet, in retrospect, his marks stand out much more strongly than do those of other writers.

The Daring Young Man has a pervasive "song-of-myself" quality. There are catalogues and passages of incantation, as when Saroyan sings of "this earth, the face of one who lived, and the deep song of man." In the beginning of the title story, Saroyan's writer, like Whitman's poet, has gathered up into himself all the experiences of past ages; for him, there have been "immense preparations." And this cosmic sweep is brought back in the closing lines to give the story a useful, if somewhat arbitrary, universality and at the same time to strengthen its effect of unity. In the death scene, Christian stoicism shades off into

Whitman's cosmic mysticism. It is "a lovely and soothing death" which the young man undergoes, and one is left with the thought, to use another phrase of Whitman's, that for him it was "just as lucky to die as to be born."

The "song-of-myself" strain runs further into the volume, appearing most recognizably in "Myself Upon the Earth," further elucidated in chapter three, and in "The Big Tree Coming," a prose elegy on the death of a young boy and the nameless people down through the ages who have died to make room for their successors. Although Saroyan's "I" is not generic like Whitman's—for he does not take the reader by the hand and urge him to assume what he assumes—there are indications that Saroyan wished to endow the self of his writing with representative qualities. Of all the classic American writers, Whitman was the most congenial to Saroyan's own temperament, but perhaps for this reason he was the least likely to help Saroyan overcome his worst faults. Only in "The Daring Young Man" does that which is redolent of Whitman serve to strengthen the story. Invariably, when Saroyan reminds us of Whitman, he is not at his best.

There are four pieces in *The Daring Young Man* that suggest a less stylized Damon Runyon. "Love, Death, Sacrifice and So Forth," "Among the Lost," and "Sleep in Unheavenly Peace" lack either the necessary humor or the dramatic structure to make them successful. "Dear Greta Garbo," however, is much better. It is a brief caricature of a star-struck American who, because of an absurd impulse to get himself photographed by newsreel cameras, gets involved in a fight with strikebreakers. After he has recovered from injuries, he sees himself on the movie screen and writes to Miss Garbo to ask that she help him begin a career in pictures. Regarded as banal by reviewers of the time, it somehow appears better now. Saroyan never intentionally falsified his people, as did Runyon; and, in his desire to catch their true speech, he is closer to Ring Lardner, though of course he lacks Lardner's scorn. Indeed, it was an awareness of man's frailties and follies that helped inspire Saroyan's affection for the individual. The image of the daring young man on the flying trapeze, with its rich connotations, stays in the reader's mind throughout the entire volume, serving as a commentary on such characters as this star-struck American, and bearing implications too for the spirit of the age in which the taste for the glamor and lavishness of movie queens contrasted sharply with its economic perils, sparseness, and violent strikes.

IV *The Changing Critical Climate*

To appreciate the impact of this first book when it appeared some thirty years ago we must try to recover a way of looking at literature which prevailed before the New Criticism, with its emphasis upon craftsmanship and formal analysis, had become the most pervasive influence in modern literature. By a coincidence which in retrospect appears somewhat ironic, the year of *The Daring Young Man,* 1934, also saw the appearance of the Henry James issue of *Hound and Horn,* a publication which proved to be of major importance in the emergence of a critical view that in some of its most characteristic aspects is inimical to Saroyan's kind of writing.[12] Developing a Jamesian conception of fiction, the New Critics began to create in this country during the late 1930's and 1940's a rather general predilection for separating the individual work of literature from the man and milieu out of which it grew in order to concentrate more fully on close textual study. By mid-century this new movement in criticism, disseminated principally through the colleges and the little magazines, had reached a rather large body of readers whose enthusiasm for its brilliant achievements, justifiable though it was, led at times to an excessively doctrinaire reaction against those writers whose work does not lend itself readily to this new kind of textual study.

But those qualities of *The Daring Young Man* which now appear somewhat intractable—its persistent autobiographical flavor and its brash profession of indifference to fiction as an art—were not incompatible to tastes of the early 1930's, nor would they have seemed especially intrusive to the many readers who responded favorably to the fictional self-portraits of two consciously unliterary writers, Sherwood Anderson and Thomas Wolfe. In a witty Aesopian fable, "The Wolfe and the Saroyan," which Clifton Fadiman wrote for the *New Yorker,* the Wolfe, jealous of his particular domain, warns the newcomer against encroachment. Undeterred but respectful, Saroyan replies: "I realize that you are a very large Wolfe and that I am a very small Saroyan, but surely the Cosmos is big enough for two of us."[13] It was big enough for these two. Horace Gregory related their phenomenal success to the psychological needs of the depression era, speculating that "at a moment when people did not trust themselves to speak aloud, it was good to have someone else, someone like Thomas Wolfe and William Saroyan, assert a vigorous, inflated personality."[14]

Sherwood Anderson helped prepare the way for both these men. In the *Saturday Review of Literature,* (October 20, 1934), William Rose Benét observed: "There is nothing either blatant or meretricious about young Mr. Saroyan's writing. There is simply his intense curiousness about life, such curiousness as was possessed by the earlier Sherwood Anderson."[15] It is true, as Burton Rascoe and Edmund Wilson also noted, that Saroyan reminded one of Sherwood Anderson; and one ought to recall, too, that the older writer presented to the literary world of the 1930's a kind of legendary exemplification of "the artist as folk-inspired amateur,"[16] thus helping immeasurably to dispose it favorably toward talented young mavericks like Saroyan.

And there were more urbane influences in the criticism of the day which helped establish a favorable reception for this new writer. Malcolm Cowley's *Exile's Return,* a book which expressed the spirit of repatriation which many intellectuals were beginning to experience after their long immersion in the European life of the post-war era, was also published in 1934. The newly awakened interest in American materials and voices which accompanied this reaction helped engender a mood which spread far beyond this immediate group of repatriates. By this time, too, the implications of Edmund Wilson's *Axel's Castle,* which had appeared three years earlier, were making themselves felt in the growing confidence of Americans in the value of their own literature and in their developing preference for social and political, rather than belletristic, aspects of literature. "The world of the private imagination in isolation from the life of society seems to have been exploited and explored as far as for the present was possible" Wilson said, insisting that the artist could no longer be set apart from the world of ordinary men.[17] Not only were Americans beginning to grant their writers the maximum freedom of expression—Edmund Wilson lent a kind of scholarly sanction to this tolerance by underscoring the changes which had come about in traditional ideas of logic in language—but they were also beginning to accept without condescension or apology the validity of an author's particular environment.

Moreover, Saroyan gained an initial advantage from two crucial controversies which reached their peak of turbulence during the early 1930's. The rear-guard struggle of the neo-Humanists in behalf of traditional standards steadily gave way before the increasingly vocal advocates of innovation and esthetic rebellion. The growing reaction against gentility and restraint was strengthened from many sources, not the least of whom was Sinclair Lewis, who gave it his heightened prestige as the first American recipient of the Nobel Prize by declaring in his celebrated Stockholm address of December, 1930, that America's literary future was in the hands of those who had the power to go their own way. With the growing social and political tensions of the depression era, however, the most characteristic critical controversy turned inevitably to the relationship of literature to economics. By 1934, men like V. F. Calverton and Granville Hicks had helped create an inordinate sensitivity to the ideological uses of literature. Whether or not one shared the Marxian views of Calverton and Hicks, the controversial atmosphere made it virtually impossible not to magnify the significance of the social protest in Saroyan's book. Many were encouraged by the author's obvious disdain for acquisitive processes in general to hope that he would prove a valuable recruit to the leftist cause. Even as it became increasingly clear that Saroyan would never conform to organized programs nor submit to group pressures, his writing continued to receive attention from those contentiously involved in this momentous controversy.

I have given considerable attention to this first book, and especially to its title story, not only because it brought Saroyan his nation-wide reputation but also because the image of the daring young man appealed so strongly to a harried and depressed nation. After some thirty years it remains indelibly imprinted in our memories, epitomizing the author and reminding us of the precarious times in which we were passing from the greatest depression into the greatest war we have ever known. In continuing to stand as an identifying epithet for Saroyan, this image helps keep alive the record of his initial reputation, but it has the disadvantage too of linking him to writing that is not his best.

CHAPTER 2

San Francisco Beat

AS WITH MANY FIRST BOOKS, reviewers had been willing to overlook the faults of *The Daring Young Man on the Flying Trapeze* because of its great promise. One would not expect this kind of immunity for a second book, however. Yet *Inhale and Exhale,* a collection of short stories which appeared two years later, managed to extend this prevailing attitude of hopeful expectancy: the *New Yorker,* the *Saturday Review of Literature,* the *New Republic, Scribner's,* and the New York *Times,* despite reservations, counted themselves among its supporters. Their reservations were strongly felt, sometimes betraying impatience, but their affirmations were equally positive. Nothing is more indicative of Saroyan's power to involve his reader than the apparent inclination toward superlatives, even when these superlatives carried equivocal implications: *Esquire* found him "incomparable"; *Scribner's,* "the most sharply edged personality who has appeared in American writing since the early Hemingway"; the *New Yorker,* "the greatest hit-and-run writer in the history of American letters"; and the *Saturday Review of Literature* went back one hundred and twenty-five years to Lord Byron to find a comparable "proud intensity" and "triumphant self-assertion."[1]

Even predominantly adverse reviews of *Inhale and Exhale,* such as Horace Gregory's in the *Herald Tribune* and Louis Kronenberger's in *The Nation,* had the effect of spotlighting the newcomer. The former called the sudden enthusiasm for Saroyan "a mindless cult with a 'true confession' element thrown in," a view which, however disparaging, encouraged one to ponder the cultural phenomenon of Saroyan's fame and to speculate about whether he would ever become a meaningful symbol for his society. The latter scolded Saroyan for not husbanding his natural gifts: "for in a field where there is not enough talent to go around, a man with the talent of Saroyan must be implored not to squander it."[2]

By this time excitement over Saroyan had reached an extraordinary pitch. Editors were vying for new material, and his first book was well into its fifth edition, a remarkable achievement in a land where collections of short stories rarely go beyond first editions. Responding to this popularity, reviewers of *Inhale and Exhale* tended to direct their attention more to the general impact of Saroyan than to the particular qualities of his new book. Though for the most part they were willing to accredit him with capabilities sufficient to account for his extensive following, it is clear that they did not wish to succumb to the persuasiveness of a popular fad. Saroyan was bad news for reviewers, as the *New Republic* admitted,[3] and one notes the tendency to rely on witticisms as a substitute for evaluations. Some were irritated by his "vacuous generalities about life and art and society and economics," as the New York *Times* put it;[4] but there was general recognition that he possessed genuine gifts and that annoyance could quickly turn to pleasurable surprise. One feels that the annoyance was strong, not because the book was so bad, but because it was potentially so good. Clifton Fadiman no doubt spoke for most of these reviewers when he said: "While I can't join the cult lock, stock, and barrel, I will cheer as violently as anyone for this surprising young Near-Eastern Far Westerner."[5]

I Inhale and Exhale

Inhale and Exhale never equaled the popular success of its predecessor; and, for reasons which will presently be discussed, it must be judged a failure. Yet going back to it now, one need not find fault with the generous concessions of the reviewers. Its most notable characteristic is the apparently spontaneous ease with which it evokes memorable scenes and leaves one with the sense that its author possessed extraordinary reserves of story material. Unlike *The Daring Young Man*, its worst problems could have been solved by the simple expedient of abridgment. Although much too long—it is the longest and on the whole the least readable of Saroyan's books—its good stories are more plentiful and much better than those of *The Daring Young Man.* Notwithstanding Saroyan's continued scorn for what he called the trickery of art, he was searching for a storyteller's technique, and his second book represents an unmistakable advance in craftsmanship.

Saroyan was sensitive to charges that he could write only about himself. But, if his first book had taught him anything, it was the importance of developing the materials of his own experience; for he dedicated *Inhale and Exhale* to "the English tongue, the American earth, and the Armenian spirit" and organized its stories very generally according to the pattern of his own life. Its movement is from boyhood in a small town to young manhood in the city and, finally, to travel abroad. The town is Fresno, though it is nameless; the city is principally San Francisco. Saroyan never identifies himself as the focal point of these stories, however. In Fresno he gives his family an Italian or Russian name, and in San Francisco he writes of a motley group of characters. But they are all more or less projections of himself; and, unlike parts of *The Daring Young Man,* it seems unimportant that he disguise his presence. Indeed, the stories are usually better when the characters are more easily identifiable as Saroyan himself. The trip to Europe which makes up the final section confirms this autobiographical base. It serves to broaden his view of man and intensify his awareness of his own cultural past.

In Rostov, Russia, late one night he came upon an Armenian waiter in a tavern.[6]

> Vy, said [the waiter] with that deliberate intonation of surprise which makes our language and our way of speech so full of comedy. You?
>
> Meaning of course I, a stranger. My clothes, for instance. My hat, my shoes, and perhaps even the small reflection of America in my face.
>
> How did you find this place?
>
> Thief, I said with affection, I have been walking.

Saroyan's heart was warmed by this unexpected encounter, for in the gestures of "this black Armenian from Moush" he saw the vigor and humor of his people and the irrepressibility of their spirit:

> The slapping of the knee and roaring with laughter. The cursing. The subtle mockery of the world and its big ideas. The word in Armenian, the glance, the gesture, the smile, and through these things the swift rebirth of the race, timeless and again strong, though years have passed, though cities have been destroyed, fathers and brothers and sons killed, places forgotten, dreams violated, living hearts blackened with hate.
>
> I should like to see any power of the world destroy this race, this small tribe of unimportant people, whose history is ended, whose wars have all been fought and lost, whose structures have crumbled, whose literature is unread, whose music is unheard, whose prayers are no longer uttered.

In these brief but strongly felt lines to his vanishing nation one can detect the primary source of an elegiac spirit which runs throughout the book, representing a development of one of the most promising aspects of *The Daring Young Man,* that expressed especially in "Seventy Thousand Assyrians." The restlessness and yearning that suffuse the stories of *Inhale and Exhale,* even those of his boyhood days in Fresno, gain depth and validity by this association with an irrevocable national past. Though it was a theme which he would soon understand better and handle with greater unity of effect, it nevertheless gave to his second book a mood that must have found responsive hearts among the many Americans who had known discontinuity in their family heritage. It was this poignant awareness of uprooting and change, I think, that instilled in Saroyan his reverence for the value of the moment and for the resilience of the human spirit. Unfortunately, it is not until the final section of *Inhale and Exhale* that he provided his reader with this emotional backdrop, and thus it is a book which gains immeasurably as one reflects back upon it.

Saroyan's answer to those who found his fiction intrusively autobiographical lay in the generic aspect of his own experience which he strove to impart to his second book. The life he wrote about was in a very real sense representative of the American earth and the old-world spirit: in these stories one finds Russians, Italians, Swedes, Poles, Mexicans, and Japanese, as well as native-born Americans set adrift by unemployment; but all are discovering the emotional cost of finding their way in a world quite different from that of their parents. Indeed, the theme which runs through the entire collection, suggesting the most fundamental reply to critics of his autobiographical manner, is that racial or economic difference, or differences of age, do not alter the fact that essentially all human beings are the same: all are destined to brief lives of pathetic and often amusing inadequacy. And the reader is constantly aware of the theme's implication that to understand this common bond is to realize the absurdity of exploiting one's fellowmen and enslaving oneself in the pursuit of insubstantial distinctions of wealth and social position.

As with his first book, the theme was timely. It suited current fashions in the literature of revolt, but those who hoped for leftist support were disappointed. The book was not Marxist. One of its few satirical pieces focused humorously on the unenlightened self-interest of two American Communists, and elsewhere there were scornful references to "the blind certainty" of Russia and her dreams of "the dictatorship of the proletariat."[7] *Inhale and Exhale* was disdainful of ideology that undervalued the individual and contemptuous of violence, especially when organized by governments; it advanced no political philosophy, and was in no way rebellious. What troubled Saroyan was man's tendency to submerge himself in his acquisitive instincts. "His attitude," observed the New York *Times*, "has nothing of the Socialist in it. He is much closer to St. Francis in his passion for freedom from the obligations of possessions."[8] In this respect he reminds one of Henry David Thoreau's assertion that we are wealthy in proportion to the number of things we can do without. The real timeliness of Saroyan's theme lay in the fact that the triumph of simply being alive was a much-needed message in 1936 when a great many depression-weary Americans knew what it meant, in Thoreau's words, to keep their accounts on their thumbnail.

The main theme is supported by motifs which set off each of the three major groupings of material. In the stories of boyhood, which will be discussed in the following chapter, the author frequently reminds us of the wider world beyond the confines of Fresno, at times to suggest the possibility of eventual escape from poverty and limited horizons but more often to imply that basically man's struggles are everywhere the same. In the stories of young men which make up the second and largest portions of *Inhale and Exhale,* loneliness and restlessness—one cannot say searching—dominate. The city does not offer them love or security, but they have left their homes and cannot return. One of them tries to go back, only to discover that, although he feels affection for his people, he can never re-enter their lives in any real sense. A young man of Russian parentage, he has absorbed enough of American life to feel an almost unbridgeable gap between himself and his family; but he is still irresistibly drawn to his folk, and sight of his old neighborhood creates in him a flood of feeling. Saroyan endows him with strong emotions and a sharply observant eye, but he wisely denies him the power to understand or even to comment abstractly on his dividedness. Thus, unencumbered by general reflections, the story conveys its strength and logic through vivid images.[9]

In "The Younger Brother," a youth of Italian parentage, having left the family home in Fresno to work in a furniture warehouse in San Francisco, realizes that with the death of his mother and father he has lost not only his home and parents but also his one vital link with their Italian past. Only in retrospect does he recognize how much their European experience has enriched his own life. An epistolary story filled with self-pity and narcissism, it at times is too obviously addressed to a third reader. But its emotional tone is appropriate, and we feel the youth's sudden awakening to separation and loneliness.

Saroyan's continuing search for a style of his own, though apparent throughout the book, is especially notable in this second grouping of stories. Those that tell of the idlers who cluster about the Kentucky Pool Room suggest that Saroyan had spent more time in the public library than in the bar or gambling room, for they read at times like a less sardonic Ring Lardner and on occasions like Damon Runyon. When Saroyan turns to the valley setting for a story of a seventeen-year-old Mexican who is killed by strikebreakers, one thinks of John Steinbeck. The title—"With a Hey Nonny Nonny"—is characteristically Saroyan, of course, and he was even then beginning to develop its setting into a domain of his own. But the story is undistinguishable from much of the proletarian literature of the period—as the reader sees, for example, in his vague and angry references to some all-powerful force in the country, the "they" of the story, that exploited the poor worker with full and malicious intent. Saroyan never learned to handle the story of social protest. Not prominent in *Inhale and Exhale,* it disappears entirely from later books.

He was much better at the kind of story Ben Hecht was then making popular. "Our Little Brown Brothers the Filipinos" tells of a two-hundred-and-fifty pound Philippine wrestler who refused to throw a match with a Russian. When the referee, cooperating with the fixers, gave the fight to his obviously outclassed opponent, the enraged Filipino threw everybody out of the ring, including the police who were sent in to subdue him, and refused to leave the ring until he was declared winner. As one reviewer noted, this is the kind of story on the fringe of the news which a city editor would block off as "human interest."[10] It shows a fine sense of the ridiculous, a style of sufficient rapidity and ease to give both humor and pathos to a subject of strong current interest. Saroyan could have found a comfortable niche for himself in the world of popular journalism had caricature ever engaged his full attention.

But Saroyan was not interested in this kind of writing, and humor is rare in *Inhale and Exhale.* For the most part, its characters are hounded by unemployment, poverty, and even hunger. Bewildered, frightened, or angered, they often seek the distractions of brothels and gambling rooms. Yet they are not really susceptible to corruption, for they possess some inner source of strength that holds them superior to their surroundings. The effect at times is to weaken our faith in the reality of his settings; but in his more convincing moments Saroyan succeeds in increasing our respect for the inviolability of the individual. In this immunity of his characters lies the most fundamental difference between Saroyan and the Naturalists to whom he owes so much. To use the subject and often the style of the Naturalists and yet to express a view of man contrary to theirs involved him in a particularly difficult problem, for Saroyan's faith in the individual seemed arbitrary and even contradictory to sensibilities shaped by the tenets of Naturalism.

Saroyan's early work reflects the influence of Sherwood Anderson more than that of any other of his contemporaries. To read in sequence stories of lonely people who seek the solace of love, a type of fiction in which Anderson's influence was especially strong, is to watch Saroyan's gradual discovery of his own strength.[11] "Secrets in Alexandria" tells of the dreary loneliness of a young man and woman who live in the same neighborhood in San Francisco and seek escape and fulfillment in the same movies; but, through his reticence, they never come to know each other. The background is effectively established through references to popular movies and newspaper headlines. The days of Marion Davies and Mae West, of the Japanese war, the rise of the Nazis, and the emergence of Franklin Delano Roosevelt flash before the reader's mind, and the city is sharply visualized. But the characters themselves never really belong here; their proper setting is Winesburg, Ohio.

"At Sundown," too, is a hybrid, although Saroyan's independence asserts itself more strongly. In it, two young lovers attend concerts and movies together and take long walks through the city. But they separate in unspoken conviction that they must accept "a less magnificent but more plausible" order of existence. Despite a surface resemblance to the frustration of many of Anderson's people, their emotional problem is fundamentally different. She is the daughter of a Russian tailor who has settled in San Francisco, and he is Austrian. Their sense of not belonging anywhere on God's earth reflects an ethnic uprooting much more immediate and thoroughgoing than that felt by Anderson's first- and second-generation Americans of the Middle West. Like so many of Saroyan's characters, what they suffer is not frustration but a melancholy too deep to be relieved by American corrective measures—not by psychoanalysis and certainly not by escaping from a suffocating environment. Unlike Anderson's fiction, there is nothing in the locale that contributes to their inability to find fulfillment. The city itself offers charm and excitement, and the girl's father receives the suitor graciously. But Saroyan's stance throughout is much like that of Anderson, and his story ends in that paradoxical negation which so often accompanies Anderson's tales of love and passion.[12] Its setting, tone, and events are much too tangible for its theme; in effect, the essential conflict must be inferred from material given elsewhere in the book.

Although "Secrets in Alexandria" is more clearly motivated, "At

Sundown" is potentially stronger, for it touches a theme close to Saroyan's own experience: the uprootedness of the immigrants and their children. "A Night of Nothing," however, presents a resolution that departs significantly from Anderson, for in this story the lovers are not cut off from each other by their need. A young man buys hamburgers and coffee for a girl who has no money; and, upon learning that she has no place to sleep, offers his room for the night. Actually, he is motivated by a disinterested pity and does not treat her like the "pick-up" she has become. Though the incident ends in sexual intimacy, the focus is not on sex. Out of her desperate need and his kindness arises a mutual respect. Though this development appears somewhat incongruous in an encounter so brief and circumstantial, it is made plausible, first, by a close link between the actions of the young people and the general atmosphere of desperation which characterizes their milieu—the sketch opens with a description of marathon dancers in an advanced stage of exhaustion—and, secondly, by a bedroom scene, more domestic than romantic, which presents the two as pathetic youngsters, lost and weary. Moreover, the story's title and the opening description serve to associate their plight with the futility of the marathon dance.

In setting, subject, and tone, "A Night of Nothing" resembles the Naturalistic literature of the time. "Two Days Wasted in Kansas City," with an equally tawdry setting, has an unexpected shift in emphasis which reveals a growing independence in its author. This story dramatizes the consciousness of an itinerant gambler who ascribes a sudden burst of luck at the dice table to the presence of a strange girl. When she slips away from the gambling room, he searches frantically for her in the belief that his winnings might save her from becoming a streetwalker. However arbitrary and naïve his conjecture may appear about the unknown girl, it exists as an integral part of his religion of luck—a faith which has been freshly renewed by the seemingly miraculous turn of the dice. But the story does not ask us to concur in a gambler's mystique or a young man's romantic intuition, for these are absorbed in his new conviction that evil comes from loss of faith in the essential worth of the individual. He is deeply disturbed by the thought that he will never have a chance to share his insight with the girl. The idea takes on unexpected cogency and force through the emotional reactions of this young gambler. The title functions ironically, for the point of the story is that, without this faith, what is wasted is nothing less than a human life. In style, manner, and theme, this is truly Saroyan's story.

Somewhat similar to these four in theme, "The Christmas Carol" and "The Mother" are also entirely in Saroyan's manner. They tell of a young man who plays good Samaritan to a girl in need—in the first, to a cousin who is spending Christmas alone in a dingy room and, in the second, to an unmarried expectant mother. In "The Christmas Carol" Saroyan asks us to share the emotional atmosphere without presenting us with the conflict itself, and thus his story is arbitrary and sentimental. But "The Mother" builds to a fine moment of recognition when two lonely people experience an illuminating awareness of the essential nobility of the other. By adroitly selecting details of setting and character, Saroyan conveys in this brief, simple tale a valid, moving sense of life. From "Secrets in Alexandria" through "The Mother"—a sequence that reveals a growing awareness of his own materials—we see clearly that Saroyan would never be a competent derivative writer. For better or worse, he would have to be judged as an independent.

The section relating to Saroyan's trip abroad discards any attempt to project themes into fiction and becomes a kind of traveler's notebook. Though an occasional sketch borders on fiction and one of its pieces, "Black Tartars," has the flavor of folklore, for the most part this section simply asserts directly the themes that have been implicit throughout the book. This material emphasizes particularly the author's conviction that life is a gift to be revered and his scorn of those things that deny the preciousness of this gift. Though Saroyan's intention was to reveal the universal relevance of these themes, by attempting too much he destroyed the unity of the book.

And there are other ways in which the great length weakens *Inhale and Exhale.* Throughout the whole book, pieces of genuine value are mixed in with incredible banalities. Saroyan's penchant for prefaces proved especially disastrous. He was probably encouraged in this habit by the example of Thomas Wolfe, whose phenomenal popularity at the time was receiving further impetus from his second novel, *Of Time and the River* (1935). Wolfe liked the rhapsodic prose preface, and in his fiction he strove to create an all-inclusive fictionalized self, projecting in a loose, rambling structure his own movement from home town to city and finally to Europe in search of cultural roots. This pattern, as previously pointed out, is fundamental to *Inhale and Exhale*. As writers, Saroyan and Wolfe had much in common: their autobiographical impulse, their indifference to form, their tendency toward exhortation, and their power to establish scene and create mood. But Saroyan was not intense, impassioned, gigantic, like Wolfe. Nor was he a searcher. Perhaps for this reason he was less tempted than Wolfe to seek the image of America in himself. But he did make the mistake of following Wolfe into the philosophical poses which mar Wolfe's work and nearly destroy *Inhale and Exhale*.

On the natural structure of *Inhale and Exhale* Saroyan has superimposed a nine-fold division, each with title and essay. The titles are a distraction and the essays are for the most part pseudo-philosophical in the worst vein of *The Daring Young Man*. They are based on a vague, indiscriminate assumption that only a mind untouched by formal education is capable of genuine and exciting insights, and on a hostility toward formal learning that deteriorates at times into a distrust of informed, disciplined thought. At best the essays are repetitive, merely specifying themes that are developed in the fiction, particularly those about the miraculous nature of life and the sanctity of the individual. But they also reveal a mood of disenchantment. And with this mood we come to the fundamental weakness of the essays, for it runs counter to the affirmation and love that is essential to his best work, even to his elegiac passages which presuppose affirmation. Saroyan had to decide which was truer for him, denial or affirmation. As we shall see, his own instinct toward affirmation was to win through. But there were persuasive influences to the contrary, and the essays of *Inhale and Exhale* suffer by this dividedness.

II Three Times Three

Saroyan's next book grew out of a casual conversation which he had with four university students who came to call on him one day in November, 1936, when he was in Hollywood working on scenarios for Ben Schulberg. Quite spontaneously and in good-natured defiance of the formalities of professional publishing, he and his visitors decided to form their own publishing company. Saroyan went to his files and brought out a sheaf of unpublished manuscripts from which nine were selected—over his mild protest a tenth, "Subway Circus," was rejected by his youthful Board of Directors. And, before a month had passed, *Three Times Three*, complete with a preface and other introductory comments, was issued by the newly formed Conference Press, Westwood Village, Los Angeles. "Something in this world's got to be uncommercial and easy-going," Saroyan said in his introduction, "and I figure it might as well be writing and publishing."[13]

The venture was a pleasant *jeu d'esprit*, one which reflected Saroyan's generosity of spirit; but few authors, if any, could afford such easy-going amiability in the making of their books. The casualness of his general introduction seemed to belie the growing respect for writing as a discipline which had begun to be evident in his recent fiction—and in what he was even then doing for later publication. Instead of reworking the old manuscripts, he prepared introductory notes for them, nonchalantly conceded the defects of his stories, and thus opened a private workbook, as it were, to the general public. Moreover, these commentaries gave the book a rather curious incongruity, for they expressed ideals of technique and form that were ignored or implicitly denied by the unfinished, often amorphous, compositions themselves.

The two most remarkable of these, "The Man with the Heart in the Highlands" and "The Living and the Dead," will be discussed in chapter three, for they belong to his Fresno material. But one piece should be mentioned here because it shows that Saroyan was developing a stronger interest in belletristic aspects of literature than is generally realized. "Public Speech" is an ironic parody of an orator; in form and intention it suggests "The Prize Day Address" of W. H. Auden's *The Orator;* and it contains such an unlooked-for literary exercise as an extended paraphrase of Chaucer's "Pardoner's Tale," which the radical orator adapts to his purpose by identifying his three ill-fated discoverers of treasure as Andrew Mellon, John D. Rockefeller, and J. P.

Morgan. The story was not without favorable notice at the time, but I am inclined to believe the approval related not to its satire but to the strong feeling for the underprivileged which lay beneath its surface. At any rate, with the passing of the depression era, it lost its principal source of appeal. Despite rather obvious similarities to Auden's piece, which had appeared in England in 1932 and in this country in 1934, where it was widely discussed and highly admired, the question of influence is of mild interest only. Because of temperament and qualities of mind, Saroyan was unlikely to absorb Auden's more incisive, subtler, and much more learned manner. We can apply to "Public Speech" what Auden later said of his own: " 'a fair notion fatally injured,' one of that painful class of good ideas which incompetence or impatience prevented from coming to much."[14] Its primary value for Saroyan was that it helped him measure the limits of his talent; for, though he possessed the ironic sense, his satiric instincts were softened by sympathy. To his credit, he never again attempted formal satire.

Three Times Three stands as a pivotal book in Saroyan's development. By-passing the professional publisher had at least one beneficial consequence: it forced the author to assume something of the editor's point of view. It was with unprecedented objectivity that Saroyan looked back over old manuscripts for his new book, and in the introductory notes he expressed a new critical awareness. He acknowledged that too often he had merely set forth the raw materials of a story, leaving his reader the task of drawing out the implied form, and thus "reversing the normal order of things." He recognized the difference between talking about life and re-creating it, and in this recognition we can see the promise of a new determination to do the artist's work. The difference, he said, is form; "and form is our only truth, or noblest objective in art and in life." For the first time, he testified to the importance of structure, of wholeness, of unity, of allowing the narrative to do its own work without the intrusive use of authorial comment. He was willing to accept the idea of himself as a teller of tales: "Critics are happiest with my stuff, I think, when I try for almost nothing, when I sit down and very quietly tell a little story. In a way, I don't blame them. I myself enjoy writing and reading a very simple story, that is whole and with form."[15]

Moreover, he no longer sounded like Walt Whitman, or Sherwood Anderson, or Ernest Hemingway, and for one moment only he reminds us again of Thomas Wolfe: "This book is a single chapter in the one book I am writing and shall have written in my lifetime. It may even be no more than a single page of that book, inasmuch as I myself cannot now determine the ultimate relationship of this small book to that larger one, or know, with any degree of finality, the variety or length or form of that larger one."[16] He knew of course that other American writers were speaking in and through him, as one may see from his sketch, "The Russian Writer" of *Peace, It's Wonderful;* but, having absorbed these influences, it was his own voice that spoke. And the writing that he was even then doing for later publications makes clear that he had evolved a style of vigor and swiftness, a style that seems conversational and colloquial in its simplicity and ease, but is actually the result of extensive and self-conscious experimentation.

The stories of 1937 and 1938 are the best to date. Not only is their style well suited to their purpose, but commentary is submerged and narrative is allowed to speak for itself. Saroyan has learned to keep his collections short, to unify the stories about a central theme, and to objectify his moods in narrative and incident. As he learned to establish an "objective correlative" for his emotions and ideas, we are able to detect an unmistakable movement toward the dramatic form.[17]

III Love, Here is My Hat

Three Times Three was followed in 1937 by *Little Children,* which will be discussed in chapter three. *Love, Here is My Hat and Other Short Romances* (1938) is the first book of which it can be said that the whole is better than any of its parts. We can read through its twenty-one stories from first to last with a growing awareness that its individual pieces are variations, consistently effective, on a meaningful theme. Taken together, they leave an impact that far exceeds that of any one of its stories. Moreover, this unity and consistency were achieved not by leveling the heights but by raising the general standard through disciplined craftsmanship. Three or four of the stories, looked at individually, are among Saroyan's best.

"The Trains" conveys as effectively as "Going Home" the ambivalence of a prodigal toward his home town. But, as it relates to the general theme of the book, it takes on another dimension: It implies that only through love and understanding, in themselves unrelated to place, can one know a true feeling of belonging. In "War and Peace," which expresses the theme of loneliness as well as anything in Saroyan, a twenty-year-old Jew is angered and humiliated by what he regards as his own commonness. He resents the whimsy of nature that had denied him gracefulness of body: "There was so much magnificence and beauty everywhere and so little of it where it could mean so much." When his mother tells him to find a good girl and get married, he blurts out sullenly: "I don't know a good girl. I don't even know a bad girl."[18] The action of the story consists of nothing more than a walk which he takes through the streets of San Francisco, but it is enough to project the pathos of his isolation and to resolve his fierce struggle into at least a temporary victory as he overcomes moroseness and self-pity, accepts with dignity the conditions which life seems to have forced upon him, and turns to Tolstoy for companionship and solace.

The stories of *Love, Here is My Hat* are interrelated through the recurring thought that love is the only possible cure for the ills of mankind. Sometimes love is used in the sense of romantic attachment, as in the title story "The La Salle Hotel in Chicago" and in "You're Breaking My Heart," "A Family of Three," and "Am I Your World?" Basic to these stories is the thought that lovers can discover a reality of their own. It may be fragile and short-lived, but nevertheless it is their only available refuge from the harshness, artificiality, and tedium of the world. Despite a blasé recognition of the sexual aspects of such love, its essentially spiritual nature is suggested by the ways in which people are caught up in its mysterious powers, and are not able to will love into or out of existence. Love cannot be bargained with or exploited; it is "The one thing in life which has its beauty and magnificence in being given."[19]

At other times, as in "Saturday Night," love refers to a strength that derives from a shared awareness of man's common lot. Indeed, even the romantic stories reflect this aspect of love, particularly "You're Breaking My Heart," in which love is strengthened by acceptance of the loved one's inadequacies, and "A Family of Three," in which this notion of love seems to constitute a binding force in the family. In "The Filipino and the Drunkard" the sense of human fellowship is outraged by a drunken white supremacist who goads a terrified Filipino into killing in self-defense. The writing effectively draws upon three sources of emotion: the determined brutality of the bully, the apathy of the crowd, the terror and helplessness of the Filipino. Irony is the most illuminating link between the second of these and the others, for some of the people are offended by the drunk's profanity. If it had not been for his obvious drunkenness, no one would have noticed him. Its theme is pertinent now as it was then. On the other hand, in "Three, Four Shut the Door" an irrational mob action is prevented by a man and his son who are moved by justice but even more by genuine affection for a half-white Negro youth who is unfairly charged with house-burning. Both of these stories are told simply, swiftly, and movingly.

The one story of people who identify love with sex is a breezy tale of a father and his teen-age son of ebullient animal spirits whose interest in sex involves them in amusing antics. Its focus is on humor, not lust. The dialogue bristles with vitality and flippancy. Through aspects of the tall tale, it is related to two other stories of the collection, "Ever Fall in Love With a Midget?" and "Gus the Gambler." The first of these was later incorporated into the script of *The Time of Your Life*. "Gus the Gambler," like many of the tall tales, exploits surprise, incongruity, and a romanticized view of the rascal that gives it a kinship with the picaresque. It has a tenuous relationship to the theme of the collection, for Gus politely deserted five wives. The proper distance is gained by the use of a slightly tipsy narrator who tells the story to a rather incredulous companion in the bar.

"The La Salle Hotel in Chicago," more representative of *Love, Here is My Hat,* offers a kind of humor which we have come to regard as more characteristic of Saroyan. On the steps of the public library in San Francisco a crusty, mocking anarchist, finds himself to his own surprise coaching a young man on how to become part of the economic system he himself so strongly despises. The young man is pathetic and inept, but he has fallen in love and speaks with a purity and genuineness that dissolves hate. Loudly and profanely the anarchist urges his bewildered companion; his bluster becomes a rather lyrical and tender espousal of the rights of young love. The humor derives from the incongruity between the bluster of the anarchist and his tender espousal of young love.

In stories like "The Trains," "A Lady Named Caroline," "The Fire," "War and Peace," "Am I your World?" loneliness engulfs the individual. In this respect the book relates to what was emerging as a major theme in Saroyan: the gap between what we reach for and what we grasp. The over-all mood of the book, however, as implied in the title, is not dark or pessimistic. If love is never found, or if it is lost, we should not try to understand. Wisdom lies in acceptance. We should smoke a ten-cent cigar and study the racing sheets. Or, like the twenty-year-old Jewish boy in "War and Peace," we should turn to Tolstoy for solace.

IV The Trouble with Tigers

A character in *Love, Here is My Hat* asks: "What do [people] want, if it isn't what they can't have? What is it, if it isn't the enormity and abundance that isn't ever steadily part of this life?"[20] And the book tells how love can tease man with the hope of this abundance. *The Trouble with Tigers,* however, shifts the attention to the meaning of unfulfillment, not in the spirit of pessimism or bitterness, but in order to place the emphasis where Saroyan obviously thinks it ought to be placed: on the value of the moment, especially on the simple, unaffected response to the moment. More consciously than ever before, he strove to design a book that would feature the sudden flash of insight into the poetry of common life. To achieve this purpose, he knew, its stories would have to be read with a sense of the shortness of life and the vulnerability of the individual. Not only is man surrounded by death—the violent, organized death of war in Spain, Ethiopia, and China is in the background—but his mind is subjected to many impersonal forces, to the regimentation of fascism and communism; and the prosaic demands of a work-a-day world, crowded trolleys, dehumanized movies, the dread of poverty, the subtle corruptions of luxury, all work together to deprive him of his life-giving sensitivities and responsiveness.

The title piece, a fantasy on time and death, sets the proper tone for the stories that follow. The trouble with tigers, it seems to say, is that they are always *there!* Unseen, they follow at the heels of every man; they are death, of course, but they are also nameless fears and the sense of inadequacy which man tries pathetically to ignore or conceal. Though a mood piece, the story is obviously autobiographical; it is not an amorphous rhapsody like some of its predecessors. It has more organization and control; and, as we may gather from the title, symbols and vignettes are made to carry much of its meaning. It reveals a few surviving traces of Whitman: the young man is a writer who is unshaven and loafs on the grass; when he goes forth over the land, he knows the pain of suffering man. He alone sees the tigers at the heels of men. But Whitman is not just adapted, he is absorbed; and his influence adds richness to the title story, as it does to the pieces which follow. Saroyan's essential Romanticism has something of William Wordsworth, too, for heaven lies about these people in their infancy, and the "shades of the prison house" close about them as they lose their spontaneity and genuineness. The natural man is now behind the soda fountain or at the gasoline station.

In some of its stories delightful, essentially innocent moments are lost through self-conscious reserve. "Another Summer," for example, tells of nineteen-year-old John Cobb who comes to the office one beautiful morning in early summer, humming Gershwin's "Summertime" and feeling light-hearted. He scoots about the office on a steel-roller chair, flirts with a secretary, and tells her he would like to be in the country, swimming and naked. Of course, he is expressing mood rather than intention, for he has no car, no money, no time. But the girl is annoyed by his audacity. In the afternoon, clouds gather and it rains. The boy is once again controlled and sane. Summer has come and gone, another time of delight wasted. It is an amusing and vital whimsy. Similarly, "I Could Say Bella Bella" describes a very brief encounter at a bus-stop between a girl and a tipsy stranger.

Her concern for his welfare and his affability are made to seem appropriate and essentially good until their spontaneous responses are replaced by a restraint that has more to do with propriety and self-awareness than with innocence.

The theme of *The Trouble with Tigers* takes on more serious dimensions with "Some Day I'll be a Millionaire Myself," which tells of a married couple in San Francisco who have lost their jobs. "We used to think it was terrible," says the husband who narrates the piece, "because neither of us had a job, and all I had was about twenty dollars. It wasn't terrible, though. It was the best thing that ever happened to us."[21] Having little or no money, they took long walks through the city and found their delight in companionship and in observing people and places. When their money was gone, the young man found a job at $18.00 a week in a hardware store:

> That was two months ago, and we are now paying all debts, buying a radio, eating three meals a day, and taking in a movie a week. Once again I am a good citizen, and the world is solid and bright. . . .
>
> It's great all right. We don't get up early in the morning any more and go to Callaghan's for coffee and doughnuts and we don't talk the way we used to talk, and we are starting a bank account, and we don't go to church and sing hymns any more, and there is no more danger in the world, and no more humor, and we read every issue of *The Saturday Evening Post* from cover to cover and like it because I am working again and want to be a millionaire myself.

The effectiveness of this story is gained primarily through the expert use of narrator. Scrupulously faithful to the point of view of the young husband, the story is consciously underwritten. The young man's voice is consistent, and his thoughts are juxtaposed deftly with his memory of his wife's words. It is one of the best examples of Saroyan's ability to surprise us with an unlooked-for effect; in this story, we are given a sudden insight into the contrast between the receptivity to life which the two share in their leisure and the absorbing commercial spirit which dominates them after he gets his job.

This skillful use of narrator is also demonstrated in "The Brokenhearted Comedian and the Girl who Took the Place of his

Unfaithful Wife,"[22] a story which achieves an ironic effect through the casual, uninvolved manner of its telling. Brief and colloquial, it is a thumbnail biography of the kind we might hear in a bar: "Maybe you remember him. He was before your time, but maybe you saw him in pictures when you were a kid. He was one of the boys who used to throw pies in the old slap-stick comedies. Johnny Kilgore. He was a small guy who was funny. He used to wear a big mustache and his most famous business was to lift his eyebrows eight or nine times by way of flirting or being amazed."

Consistent with his choice of narrator, Saroyan avoided any reflective generalities on the age-old theme of the sad clown, but our inevitable fascination for the subject is represented by the devoted girl who cannot console him but cannot leave him. The briefness of this sketch creates an effect something like that of an epitaph. Its concluding lines are:

> One day he took her up in his plane while he was cockeyed. He was cockeyed most of the time. He flew out around Catalina Island and then decided to land. He came down to land and then decided to have some fun, so he turned around and shot straight up and the motor died. The plane dived straight into the ocean.
>
> I mean, that's all. They didn't find him or her.
>
> It used to scare her to death to get into the plane, but she just couldn't think of being away from him.

The keynote story of *The Trouble with Tigers* is "O.K., Baby, This is the World." The title is taken from the remarks of a doctor as he holds up an infant by the legs and slaps it into life: "O.K., Baby, this is the world, so inhale and exhale and be with us a while. They're not going to be kind to you out there because nobody was kind to them, but don't hate anybody. There's nobody to hate."[23] These words are from a movie script which the speaker in the story, a scenario writer, is engaged in brightening up for Paramount. The story opens with a taxi ride from the movie studio to the Brown Derby where the scriptwriter has a luncheon engagement with the director of the film. Amid selections of popular songs, the radio in the cab reports fragments of news: Notre Dame has lost to Army, Landon has lost to Roosevelt, the Fascists have advanced on Madrid. At lunch, the director gives an autograph to a youngster who has no idea who he is. The two men discuss ways of making a poor script acceptable. Unobtrusively, Saroyan sketches the kind of world the infant will have to join. As in the two stories discussed immediately above, Saroyan was experimenting with the type of story that seemed casual while striving for ambitious effects.

In the conversation, the director says that it is impossible to write about the people in Hollywood because he believes they are phony: "And the girls from Ohio suffer because they want to be actresses. Everything everybody wants down here is not worth suffering for." The writer says nothing: "I didn't agree, but I didn't say anything because I knew it would take me an hour to show why it is not possible for anything to be phony if one suffers for it. That isn't a subtle thing to know, but it is a difficult thing to explain." And thereby Saroyan introduces the theme which was to emerge as one of his finest: the value of suffering.

In such a world, Saroyan could retain his faith in man only by concentrating on the individual and on his personal responses. Sadness and pain were everywhere present, not as a subject but as the condition in which his people must live. Again, it is the wisdom of acceptance which he implies. But he doesn't lose his humor or his irony in sympathy, as we can see, for example, in such titles as "The People, Yes and Then Again No." Indeed, it is Saroyan's humor that saves him again and again from sentimentality. Moreover, poverty has its uses: "If you've been poor and alone in any city of the world you've known the glory of the place, and the awful reality, especially the awful reality of the faces of the people everywhere; the hungry faces and the well-fed ones; the tired ones and the refreshed ones."[24]

The book has its failures, most notably those under the heading "Woof Woof," which are essays of the kind that mar his earlier books. On the other hand, these essays are preceded by five excellent stories, the finest sequence yet to appear; and the book leaves one with the realization that Saroyan has become a disciplined artist who knows well what effects he wishes to achieve. He has learned to adapt technique and manner to his theme, to render rather than declaim his themes, as he had so often done before. He has learned to select details for a scene without slowing down the story:

> Felix came into the O.K. Lunch on Kearney Street where I was having a hamburger and a cup of coffee, and he said, Guess what happened, Fritz? I got a job.
>
> I nearly choked.
>
> The waitress came running with a glass of water and Felix slapped my back.[25]

Thus the reader is in the story immediately. Graham Greene, writing in the *Spectator*, noted that, like Pirandello, Saroyan could get the reader into a story without any of those modern equivalents of "once upon a time" and that, again like Pirandello, he could give one the sense of a story tossed off easily.[26] Saroyan does not introduce the reader to his characters, he said; they introduce themselves. Having learned to write with deliberate unpretentiousness, Saroyan could now retain the appearance of artlessness and so convey that sense of wonder which his stories often achieved. His vision seemed fresh; but his renderings were not naïve; they were consciously contrived. Those reviewers who after *Three Times Three* continued to write of Saroyan's artlessness and lack of control simply failed to notice the difference. Saroyan was a changed man, a sober, dedicated artist: all the more so because he could make being such an artist look easy.

V Peace, It's Wonderful

Peace, It's Wonderful forms a kind of trilogy with *Love, Here is My Hat* and *The Trouble with Tigers.* Like them, it is organized about a single theme. Appearing in 1939, a period of war abroad and quickening preparations at home, peace has become more elusive and the tigers more menacing than ever. Running throughout these twenty-seven stories is the implication that the wonder of peace lies in this: every man seeks it, not knowing where it is or what it is; if he finds glimpses of it at all, it is in brief moments of sympathy and understanding.

One of these moments is found in "The Greatest Country in the World," the first and probably the best story of the collection, in which a father and son are dismayed by their own helplessness in the world: the one, because of the threatened extinction of his native Czechoslovakia; the other, because he has unknowingly got involved in strike-breaking activities and been beaten by angry men. In a remarkably vital and convincing domestic scene, the father, behaving more like an older brother, wrestles with the boy. It is a vigorous fight in which furniture is overturned and dishes are broken, but the tensions are relieved. They end laughing and agreeing that men of violence won't have things so easy after all. Another of these moments is experienced by a Scandinavian dockworker who has been clubbed in a water-front strike and taken to an emergency hospital. In a casual gesture of sympathy, a brusque young doctor, after dressing the patient's wound, thrusts a dollar into his hand. This kindness is of great importance to this immigrant worker, for he is struggling to keep free of bitterness. He would keep the dollar as an important reminder: "It is money if I spend it. If I do not spend it, it is many things, maybe what we have lost and are trying to get back."[27]

But such consolations are rare in this book. In one story a family grieves for their son, an American college student, who has died fighting as a volunteer in Spain. In another, a generous but impractical grocery clerk gives fruit and vegetables to people who are too poor to pay. In a third, a young office worker on his lunch hour wistfully plays a showroom piano which he cannot afford to buy. Perhaps it is just as well that we cannot have what we want in life, he says; and then he adds, after a pause, or maybe it isn't. In a fourth, two men discover that they cannot figure out whom to blame for the mess of the world, and then they realize that they also cannot find anyone to praise. To them, one event has come to seem no worse than another. A fifth story points up the inbred snobbishness, cupidity, and sensuousness of men by telling of a model at Magnins who fights to maintain her dignity and self-respect despite the condescension of women shoppers and the insinuations of young men. She cultivates her mind by reading Plato to her dreamy boyfriend, but she finds that he is hostile to any schemes that might curb the wealth-gathering powers of the rich because one day he hopes to be among them.[28]

A fitting image of the times is the great dust storm of the Southwest as it is described in "Noonday Dark." Here Saroyan's narrator is overwhelmed by the blindness of men and the ugliness of cities. But Saroyan's heritage of Armenian Christianity makes itself felt in this sketch, for his narrator comes to realize that God can be found in these cities, that God is in man. The meaning of the book is not so much that peace is wonderful but that man is wonderful; for, though beset by evils within and without, he "stumbles mournfully after God."[29]

Though there is a uniform proficiency throughout *Peace, It's Wonderful* that is comparable to *Love, Here is My Hat* and to *The Trouble with Tigers*, it has fewer stories of note. As early as 1939, we can see signs that Saroyan would prove better able to adjust himself and his art to a depression than to a war. Moreover, he had drawn heavily on his San Francisco experience; and, with the completion of this last book, he was not to draw upon it again for a collection of short stories until 1944.

CHAPTER 3

The Valley of Home

THE IMPORTANCE of San Francisco to the young Saroyan is clear from his earliest writings. In 1928 he published a story in the *Overland Monthly and Out West Magazine* which attests to the excitement and sense of broadening horizons which came to him from the varied life of the city.[1] Though Saroyan's adopted city was the first to stimulate his creative imagination, his native Fresno and the San Joaquin Valley were to provide a deeper and, at least in respect to the short story, a more substantial stimulus.

I *Themes of Childhood and Adolescence*

"Myself Upon the Earth," from his first book, *The Daring Young Man*—an earnest monologue through which run the twin motifs of transience and the author's desire "to keep the moment solid and alive"—makes clear Saroyan's wish to discover his own identity in terms of its full Armenian-American duality. Unlike many sons of immigrants, he had no intention of rejecting the old-world elements in his background. As if to demonstrate what this acceptance could mean to him creatively, he gives us a vividly imagined vignette of his father, an old-world figure who strives to retain his individuality amid the impersonal work-a-day world of his adopted land.[2] At once pathetic and amusing, this portrait is written with remarkable sureness of touch. Indeed, it is the only worth-while passage in this otherwise amorphous, derivative piece; and it anticipates what was to become one of Saroyan's finest themes: the profound spiritual uprootedness of the immigrant.

This same sureness of touch is found too in "A Shepherd's

Daughter," also of *The Daring Young Man.* Drawing upon his own family background in a piece that makes no attempt to disguise himself, he presents his grandmother who scolds him for his inability to work with his hands: "Can you make a simple table, a chair, a plain dish, a rug, a coffee pot? Is there anything you can do?"[3] And she relates an ancient tale of a Persian prince who saved himself from thieves, married a beautiful girl, and lived happily ever after—all because he had learned to weave straw mats. Told swiftly and lightly, the legend is adapted to the personality of the old woman and remains faithful to her in tone and spirit. We feel her reality as well as that of the gap between the generations. Yet the young man's amusement is without condescension as he laughingly reasserts his own commitment to the impractical life of books.

As pointed out in chapter two, it was difficult for Saroyan in his San Francisco material to distinguish personal observations from those which came to him through books. However, as he turned back to his earlier experiences, he seemed automatically to free himself from literary influences. In the vignettes of his father and grandmother, as we have seen, he instinctively found the right tone; and, though he was not yet ready to explore their fictional possibilities, it was clear that he could visualize members of his family with a charming mixture of involvement and detachment. At the same time, his stories of adolescence were to require much hard work and experimentation before he was to discover their proper focus and tone.

In his first book, *The Daring Young Man*, the most successful of these stories of adolescence is "And Man," which combines the theme of personal isolation with that of the awakening self-awareness of an awkward fifteen-year-old boy who learns that others do not know him as he is—or as he wishes himself to be. In form of recalled experience recounted in the first person, it makes plausible and moving the boy's emotional crisis. Less successful are those stories which confront directly the sexual aspects of adolescence. The young men of "Seventeen" and "Snake" are aware of a strong ambivalence toward sex. In the first, the conflict is unresolved because the boy yields to lust without finding relief from his loneliness; in the other, a somewhat older protagonist discovers a solution in the larger meaning of shared experience. But in this story Saroyan is too detached, as in the first he is too involved, to make his story convincing. In "Love" a young fellow who visits a brothel finds he must stifle an impulse to rescue one of the girls when he sees how deftly she thwarts such attempts. But his open-eyed wonder at the harlot's nonchalance is also the author's, who thus fails to bring out the potential humor of the situation—the only possible value of an otherwise obvious, sentimental piece.

Saroyan was never at ease with these stories, less from any perceivable embarrassment than from a disinclination to acknowledge the corruptibility of his people. Sexual intimacy was caused by loneliness or sympathy, but rarely by lust, and passion was never the center of focus. His young men were at times attracted to harlots but never corrupted by them. Seventeen-year-old Sam Wolinsky is filled with disgust and self-loathing by his visit to a brothel. More characteristically, however, the prostitutes themselves are harmless, and are given an occult knowledge of human nature and an ability to undercut the phoniness of society that poorly disguise the hackneyed tradition of the brusque but good-hearted whore.[4] Another aspect of his hygienic view of low life can be seen in "The Man with the French Postcards," an awkward tale of two gamblers, hungry and down on their luck, who discover in themselves a latent sense of decency when they destroy a packet of pornographic pictures rather than peddle them for much-needed lunch money. To his credit, Saroyan soon abandoned this kind of material. These stories are basically concerned with the pathos of longing, a theme which he learned to explore more meaningfully in other contexts.

With this diffidence in writing of sexual passion, pre-puberty childhood inevitably seemed more congenial to his imagination. How instinctive this preference was can be seen in his story of John Melovich, who learns that his girl is two months pregnant. The story turns on the young man's decision to accept his responsibilities, but his mind keeps slipping back to early childhood, and visions of his family nearly supplant his awareness of the girl and the conditions of their love affair. These flashbacks are presented impressionistically in a style which Saroyan never mastered and later abandoned, but they leave the reader with a new appreciation for the presentness of the past. The only story in *The Daring Young Man* which directly concerns a young child has many of the virtues that Saroyan achieved in his stories of adults only after much more time and effort. In "Laughter," the setting and situation are established effortlessly and the characters have vitality. Yet it has a serious flaw, one that points out a difficult technical problem which Saroyan faced with this kind of story: how to imply mature meanings without intruding the mature self. It tells of a ten-year-old Italian-American schoolboy who is punished for laughing aloud in class. But his laughter, closely bound up with what people cry about, is like that described in the Preface to *The Daring Young Man*, and the youngster cannot be made to carry such a burden of maturity.

Stories of boyhood in *Inhale and Exhale* show Saroyan's continued concern with this problem. "The World and the Theatre" never achieves a clear focus because the comments of the central figure, a newsboy who sells his papers across from the theater, often sound like the author. But "London, Ah London" is more successful in this respect. Eleven-year-old Nathan, a Jewish schoolboy who is completely dissatisfied with his life in the small American town, dreams of escaping to this faraway city which he knows from reading *Oliver Twist*. But this time, Saroyan allows his boy only relatively slight intimations of the ethnic differences which are complicating his life, and thus he implies more than could be directly stated about the improbabilities, as well as the importance, of Nathan's dreams.

Despite weaknesses of style, these stories reveal a steady growth in technical competence, particularly in the way they comment on what was beginning to emerge as a dominant theme: the inability of man to fulfill his aspirations, a theme which Saroyan was learning to present poignantly from a boy's angle of vision. His Italian newsboy shouted out headlines as he hawked his papers across from the theater; and, by force of repetition, their images of ugliness, suffering, and failure lodged themselves painfully in his consciousness. Poverty in his own home made him particularly susceptible to human problems everywhere.

But these stories were not written in the spirit of adult sympathy for underprivileged children, and they do not dichotomize society into adults and children. Saroyan knew well the dangers of poverty to youngsters, but he also realized that paradoxically hardship could heighten their responsiveness to experience and draw them closer to their families. The newsboy often went to the movies after selling his papers, usually sneaking by the ticket-taker to save an additional dime for his contribution to the family food box. When he arrived home late, his mother would watch him with sympathetic understanding as he ate the soup she had kept warm on the back of the stove. And other memorable vignettes illustrate this unity of feeling between children and their elders. We who have known the soporific effects of almost unbroken prosperity may regard such scenes as sentimental, but readers of the 1930's rarely thought them so. Saroyan, who knew this kind of life, wrote of it with genuine feeling.

The conflict in the stories turns not on an adult-child polarity but contradictory impulses of the human heart, often reflecting the animosities and prejudices which children absorbed from their elders. "The War," for example, tells of a group of boys who are goaded by strong anti-German feeling into beating up a hapless German boy in their neighborhood. The youth who reports the incident is fascinated by its starkness and does nothing to stop the violence; yet he is outraged by the senseless cruelty, and his recoil implicitly indicts hatred everywhere.

When there is a clash between children and adults, it usually relates to restrictions which people place on the child's simple responsiveness to nature. In "Five Ripe Pears," a little boy who steals newly ripened fruit learns that the bounties of nature are not necessarily his to enjoy. The narrator is an adult who, in recalling his own childhood, reveals a good deal of his present self, and thus the story combines a child-like view of authority with a more mature understanding of how ill-fated must be many of our happiest moments. The opening lines establish this duality effectively: "If old man Pollard is still alive I hope he reads this because I want him to know I am not a thief and never have been. Instead of making up a lie, which I could have done, I told the truth and got a licking."[5]

But these clashes reflect blindness rather than viciousness in adults; and, although Saroyan regrets their circumscribing effects, he never suggests that they leave children scarred in any permanent or ominous way. A good-natured humor plays throughout these stories, and some are merely anecdotes with a comic twist, as in "The Living Multitude," which establishes delightfully a youth's vigorous responsiveness to life only to place it in incongruous contrast to the preference of adults for comfort. He awakens at dawn one June day, trots down Ventura Avenue, slapping fence posts and swinging on sycamore branches, and goes to his cousin's home where he shouts out to the entire household that it is morning and time to be awake.

The primary weakness of these stories of *Inhale and Exhale* lies in their language, which is sometimes turgid and clumsy. By 1936 Saroyan had not yet evolved a style adequate to his subject. His dialogue lacked the flavor of common speech, and he was often strained and unnatural in trying to catch the casual profanity and coarseness of boy's talk. Moreover, his young ones tended to merge into the same personality. The opening passage of "The World and the Theatre" is a fair example of the derivative, frenzied quality of some of this work. It speaks of howling dogs and frightened eyes of people, but there is no one to hear the dogs or observe the people. In expressions like "desolating sadness," "awful clumsiness," and "the pathetic lack of poise and power," we realize that emotional words are trying to do the work of real emotions. However, when Saroyan turned directly to the Armenian moorings of this material, he immediately began to show the same sureness of touch that had characterized his earlier portraits of his father and grandmother.

II *Armenian Moorings*

In the opening passage of "The Broken Wheel," the first story of *Inhale and Exhale* which identifies the family as Armenian, he gives us, instead of attitudes and emotions, things: the small house on Santa Clara Avenue in the foreign district, a house that had belonged to a man in the business of roasting and marketing all kinds of nuts, so that nut-shells and nut-meats were wedged in the cracks of the floors. There were crickets near the kitchen sink, and a big black tomcat who came up from the darkness of the cellar. This naming of things reflects a strong power of recall and a residue of genuine emotion in the heart of the author; and, because the feeling was there, the language could be simple and unstrained.

Saroyan still had much to learn about economy in selecting details, but he had discovered an important principle. From this point on, he developed rapidly in his ability to create scenes that were both specifically visualized and richly suggestive. Through the eyes of its eight-year-old narrator we see in "The Broken Wheel" the mother, the sisters Naomi and Lucy, the older brother Krikor, and Uncle Vahan who frequently drives down from the city in his red Apperson to give them rides. Krikor, who is eleven, sells the *Evening Herald* after school and buys such unlikely things as a cornet, which he tries determinedly to play, and a bicycle so big for him that he must ride under the bar. Though brief, the story gains scope by means of an apparently trivial incident, the breaking of a bicycle wheel, which takes on an abiding significance for the boys when it becomes indelibly associated in their minds with the crushing news of Uncle Vahan's sudden death. The wheel is left unrepaired and life's joyous possibilities seem to them permanently diminished.

There are good companion pieces to this story, such as "Daily News," in which the narrator, after finally convincing Krikor and his mother that he too should sell papers after school, experiences something of the distress and uncertainty of the outside world. "The Barber Whose Uncle Had His Head Bitten Off by a Circus Tiger" is little more than an anecdote in which the boy gets the worst haircut of his life but is served coffee by an eccentric Armenian barber who tells the lad of the daring life and sudden death of his Uncle Mesak of Moush. The barber's name is Aram, and one realizes that with the Armenians of Fresno Saroyan has begun to make use of his best materials.

In "Antranik of Armenia," Saroyan projects the idyllic aspects of boyhood in a small Armenian town against a background of conquest and aggression in the world.[6] The occasion of the story is the general's visit to Fresno; it conveys intensity of feeling for Armenia harassed by Turks and subdued by Russians "in the name of brotherhood"; and it pictures Armenians in their vineyards and churches: "Their vines were exactly like the vines of California and the faces of the Armenians of Armenia were exactly like the faces of the Armenians of California." The story suggests the essential unity of mankind and points to the mysterious paradox that man is both fierce and kind. On the day of the general's arrival, the boy scrambles up a telephone pole to see the celebrated visitor above the crowds of enthusiastic Armenians who had gathered at the Southern Pacific station. He was a tall man of about fifty, very solid and strong, "in a neat American suit of clothes. . . . He had an old-style Armenian moustache that was white. The expression of his face was both ferocious and kindly. The people swallowed him up and a committee got him into a great big Cadillac and drove away with him."

But the story is about the boy and his uncle, a relationship enhanced by the grimness surrounding it:

> I got down from the telephone pole and ran all the way to my uncle's office. That was in 1919 or 1920, and I was eleven or twelve. . . .
>
> I was working in my uncle's office as office boy. All I used to do was go out and get him a cold watermelon once in a while which he used to cut in the office, right on his desk. He used to eat the big half and I used to eat the little half. If a client came to see him while he was eating watermelon, I would tell the client my uncle was very busy and ask him to wait in the reception room or come back in an hour. Those were the days for me and my uncle. He was a lawyer with a good practice and I was his nephew, his sister's son, as well as a reader of books. We used talk in Armenian and English and spit the seeds into the cuspidor.

Fresno lives vividly in these stories. We hear its "sounds of living" in fragments of popular songs, in the whistle of the popcorn wagon as it passes along Santa Clara Street, in the voices of Casparian, the melon peddler, and of Miss Gammon at the Emerson School. At the same time, by using the device of recollected narrative to combine the freshness of a boy's outlook with the knowledge and understanding of a man, Saroyan has made its image a part of a wider world in which kindness is corrupted by stupidity and the spirit of vengeance.

The two most notable pieces of his next book, *Three Times Three,* also derive from Fresno and the Armenian background. "The Man with the Heart in the Highlands" is a fantasy made tangible by the concrete language of the boy who is its narrator. In the opening line his strong sense of reality is there as anchor:

"In 1914, when I was not quite six years old, an old man came down San Benito Avenue on his way to the old people's home playing a solo on a bugle and stopped in front of our house." Though the story betrays speed of writing—Saroyan claimed to have done it in about an hour and a half—it has charm and the great merit of implying rather than stating its theme. The idea was to stay in Saroyan's mind for a long time. One of the few things he ever bothered to rework, he later developed it into one of his finest plays.[7]

If Saroyan was too relaxed with this piece, he was too ambitious with "The Living and the Dead," a story similar in theme which he tried to load with more meaning than a work of short fiction can be made to carry. Attempting a kind of "Wasteland," he combined the theme of the vigor and charm of the past as it is half-remembered, half-created in the memory of an immigrant with the theme of the spiritual poverty and squalor of the present. Although he obviously labored much harder with this story than was his custom to express this complex theme successfully, he needed either the fuller scope of the novel or the greater intensity of poetry. As it stands, he succeeded only in part. Yet what is good in this story is among the very best of his themes, and what fails stands as a testimony to his seriousness as a writer, verifying an assertion which he made in one of his introductory notes: "Maybe I'm not yet old enough to be a truly great writer, but I am certainly, likewise, not yet old enough not to want to be a truly great writer."[8]

To do the story at all, Saroyan had to project a kind of melancholy that is known to Armenians and to others who throughout the generations have tended to regard the human condition as something to be endured. It is a melancholy whose depth and pervasiveness can easily be missed by the more sanguine Americans. In casting himself as narrator and central figure, he brought the force of personal testimony to the reality of this mood and at the same time achieved a priceless intimacy in his portrayal of the grandmother who provides the story with the essential link between past and present. She clings tenaciously to her memories of her husband Melik, and she wonders why her children and grandchildren have become so unlike him. She recalls how Melik used to ride his black horse through the hills and forests of Armenia, drinking and singing, and terrifying the wild Kourds of the desert with his presence. "If he was sober," she said, "he spoke quietly, his voice rich and deep and gentle, and if he was drunk, he roared like a lion and you'd think God in Heaven was crying lamentations and oaths upon the tribes of the earth." And, when he laughed, "it was like an ocean of clear water leaping at the moon with delight."

The old woman's image of Melik becomes a kind of reference point to measure the loss of vigor and self-reliance in the modern world. Paradoxically, he is "the living"; they, "the dead." Determined not to be overwhelmed by the strangeness of her present life, the old woman must rely on her own unsophisticated wisdom and idealized memories of her husband to protect her from the loquacity and deceptive plausibility of the Communist talk to which she is exposed through her grandson's associates:

> Everybody is poor, said my grandmother. The richest man in the world is no less poor than the poorest. All over the world there is poverty of spirit. I never saw such miserliness in people. Give them all the money in the world and they'll still be poor. That's something between themselves and God.
>
> They don't believe in God, I said.
>
> Whether they believe or not, said my grandmother, it is still a matter between themselves and God.

Her own rather willful independence of spirit is reflected in a brief confession which she makes to her astonished grandson: she has stolen three packages of cigarettes from her grocer Dikranian in reprisal for his having taken advantage—intentionally, so she thought—of her unfamiliarity with American money and having short-changed her by three pennies. But she has learned to live in the presence of this Armenian melancholy, which the author calls her natural state. As her grandson leaves the house, she calls to him in her forthright way: "Boy, get a little drunk. Don't be so serious."[9]

This conversation can effectively stand by itself—it appeared in *Harper's Bazaar*, February, 1936, as "My Grandmother"—but in "The Living and the Dead" it forms part two of a four-part story. It is filled with implications about what time does to men's dreams, which Saroyan tried admirably to project through forms of contemporary American life. As the young man in the story, he visits Third Street in San Francisco, which is described as a West Coast wasteland where impoverished, angry men gather like grotesque figures in a nightmare. Vaguely and half-heartedly he is enroute to the Fillmore Street meeting of the local Communists, but under the spell of his grandmother he realizes that the tawdriness and misery of the times involve fundamental human inadequacies that are overlooked in the Communist program. Quite drunk, he staggers into their meeting and blurts out: "What good will it do when everbody has bread, comrades? What good will it do when everybody has cake, comrades? What good will it do when everybody has everything? . . . Everything isn't enough, comrades, and the living aren't alive, brothers, even the living are dead, and you can't do anything about that."[10]

But the charm of the story fades when it leaves the grandmother, and its two themes are never fused into a meaningful unit. The valuable part was perhaps too close to Saroyan for him to realize the impact it could have on others. He recognized that the story was a failure, but he seemed not to realize why: the best of it, he thought, was the drinking scenes in a San Francisco bar. Nevertheless, he understood fully what he was trying to do in this "mournful comedy," as he called it; and nowhere in his fiction of the 1930's can we find writing that so effectively anticipates the illusive beauty of *The Time of Your Life.*

The new critical awareness of which I have spoken in connection with *Three Times Three* made itself felt in the stories of 1937 and 1938. Having learned the importance of establishing equivalent images for his ideas and emotions, Saroyan turned more and more to his boyhood in search of these fictional devices as we see in *Little Children,* his next book, and in *Trouble with Tigers,* which soon followed. But, to develop this rich vein, he had to learn more about how to adjust the autobiographical base of his stories to the demands of fiction. In *Three Times Three* he asserted that one "must get beyond the physical events (which is history) to the subtlest and most evanescent of universal meanings evolving from all the facts which make for consciousness in man."[11] Out of this notion grew the realization, as his fiction would soon demonstrate, that his own personal experience was not a picture but a window opening out to a more representative truth. What was more elusive for him was the realization that the self implied in the story can never be the same as the man writing: he could never project himself fully or accurately; what got into the most autobiographical fiction was as much a product of imagination as of memory.

Saroyan need not have troubled himself about charges that he was forever re-creating his own personality. For some time criticism had recognized that the "I" of a poem, even of the most personal lyric, should never be construed as the poet himself in any faithful autobiographical sense, for to do so was to undercut the literary purpose and betray the artist whose primary aim was to illuminate the human situation. Somehow this conclusion was slow to be applied to fiction. In none of the reviews of Saroyan's work can one find a sense of this fundamental distinction. The general tendency was to assume that Saroyan forever wrote about himself. Saroyan was sensitive and responsive to criticism; and, in retrospect, we feel that more critical help in this respect may have saved him from squandering some of his finest material through lack of confidence in his own instinctive methods.

III *The Immigrant*

With the publication of *Little Children* (1937), reviewers began to speak of the new Saroyan. T. S. Matthews, for example, observed in the *New Republic* that Saroyan's latest stories were really stories this time: "They are told by a Saroyan who is less a show-off and more of a writer than he was a year ago."[12] Harold Strauss commented in the New York *Times* that "it is a very much subdued Mr. Saroyan that we have before us—and a very much more effective one."[13] Change was a keynote in other reviews, too. Looking back over Saroyan's stories with their chronological order in mind, we can see that this newness was a matter of development rather than change in the strict sense; and to account for it we need not go beyond the art of writing and the hard discipline which Saroyan had been undergoing. There is nothing in *Little Children* that surpasses the best of the Armenian portions of *Inhale and Exhale,* with the possible exception of "The Crusader" in which Saroyan draws upon his Fresno background but uses an adult as his fictional self, or

"Countryman, How do you like America?" which is about an adult of Armenian origins. These exceptions are especially germane because the stories of adults which Saroyan was doing at this time—those that appeared in *Love, Here is My Hat* and in *The Trouble with Tigers*—are almost always superior to those of adults which he had done earlier. For some reviewers the image of the daring young man so overshadowed his other creations that, when *Little Children* appeared, they seemed unmindful that the Fresno material, both in stories of childhood and in those of Armenian adults, had appeared before. And though these stories of Fresno also show a steady advancement in technical competence, the difference is not so apparent that a critic would be likely to speak of a new Saroyan. The pivotal book in his general development, as I have said before, is *Three Times Three,* and its prefatory comments say nothing that cannot be inferred from a careful reading of his stories to that time.

On the other hand, some reviewers had become vexed by the proliferation of Saroyan stories. The sins of his past, most notably his overeagerness to publish, had caught up with him. Feeling that Saroyan's typewriter was never still, many ceased to read him with care. This fact can be seen, for example, in their charge that the fictional characters of *Little Children* are all "little Saroyans." To a personality so irrepressible as Saroyan's, there would always be some truth to this assertion and it was a rather dependable, and overworked, generalization. Yet this criticism is not appropriate to *Little Children,* and it indicates that many reviewers were merely relying on earlier impressions. It overlooks the significant differentiation between the two generations represented in the book: the immigrants and their children. In the past Saroyan had sometimes deserved criticism for baldly stating his themes; but now, when he stood back and let his fiction speak for itself, some of his readers missed his meaning. It was left to an anonymous critic of the London *Times* to point out the value of its implied commentary on American life. Here is a "sharp-cut rendering of boyish minds," and it presents a great many immigrants whose children were being made into Americans: "It is a remarkable annotation of the spirit of Americanism, with its fierce theoretical equality, and its tolerance of harshest inequality, money being the measure."[14]

For the immigrant, America meant a chance to live unmolested in an atmosphere of freedom. For his children, this freedom came to mean the chance of moneymaking. The young man of "The Coldest Winter since 1854" dreams of getting a job and making money "to buy guns and fishing tackle and maybe a little Ford." His sense of competition with the boys across the tracks was more than a matter of prowess at football; and his love affair with the little rich girl in his class was amusing but in its futility suggestive of F. Scott Fitzgerald's theme of the *vampirism* of the rich.

The mysterious, immutable laws governing the lines of social demarcation are never explicitly Saroyan's subject. But his young people knew what it meant to be outsiders. In "Corduroy Pants," this meaning is explored in respect to children's brutal scorn for what is out of fashion. In "Higher Accountancy," two gifted, intelligent students achieve absolutely nothing because the mediocrity of their home environment proves virtually inescapable. Well named, it is the reverse of the American success story. Though somewhat diffuse, it raises provocative questions about the accident of birth and the pathos of wasted lives. If intelligence alone cannot break the barrier, neither can money. Indeed, paradoxically, the zest for riches, though encouraged by a fluid economy, is self-defeating for the persons involved, whatever it may mean for their descendants. And, if it becomes frenzied, as it does for Nathan Katz in "The Man Who Got Fat," it is to Saroyan an even more melancholy comment on wasted lives.

Contrary to what the title may suggest, *Little Children* is not essentially about children. Fundamentally, it makes the point that what is truly precious about childhood is not a matter of age but of freshness of spirit. Such responsiveness is forever jeopardized by the world of affairs, but the book shows us unhappy, even bitter youngsters and adults who are young in heart. Its emphasis is upon loss, and its prevailing mood is one of sadness. In "Sunday Zeppelin" two boys are fooled by the false advertising of a mail-order company, a ruse that seems especially vicious because the advertisement appears in their Sunday school paper. But the story does not romanticize its subject. The card-board zeppelin turns out to be an ersatz version of what the boys were promised, but their plans had been a source of friction between them and they had been perfectly willing to finance the purchase by withholding their dimes and nickels from the collection plate. Thus the conflict is not between innocent youth and a treacherous world; it is embedded in the human heart.

And there are other children, too, who serve as reference points for broader human conflicts. In "Many Miles per Hour," the colorful life of a speed driver is viewed through the admiring eyes of two little boys, and his sudden death plunges them into an incomprehending anger that implies a great deal about man's helplessness before the inexorable laws of caution and practicality. Man is forever dreaming and life is forever denying. A Jewish newsboy who learns this truth too soon is called "Laughing Sam." But he was not laughing, as his fellow newsboy later discovers: "It sounded like *laughing*, but he was crying."[15]

An exception to this note of sadness appears in "My Uncle and the Mexicans," which tells of a fruitworker and his family who never recognize the realities of a competitive economy or trouble themselves about social differences. Saroyan does not tell us whether in the final analysis these people are naïve or sophisticated; but, through the kindness of a rancher, they live in idyllic, if precarious, happiness. A companion piece, "Where I come from People are Polite," tells of an office boy who quits his job so that one of the older workers will not lose hers. Though fully aware of his sacrifices, he is without self-righteousness. As compensation for a pleasure excursion he must cancel, he treats himself to a motorcycle ride down the peninsula—a wild, unpremeditated defiance of all prudence for which he forfeits his last paycheck to the Harley-Davidson dealer. In the light of his uncertain future, the young man cannot understand his own ebullience. The story does not moralize; but it makes clear that, though there may be penalties for impetuosity, there is also an unmistakable connection between generosity of spirit and peace of mind.

A brief sketch that reflects the characteristic mood of the entire book is "The Cat" in which a boy and a girl visit in simple fellowship with a workman as he lays a concrete sidewalk. One of Saroyan's adults who have managed to preserve their capacity to react youthfully, he converses easily with the children. After he has finished his work, the two children engrave their initials in the soft cement and then skate off together into an uncertain future. A mood piece on the theme of mutability, it is wistful and fragile, and in no way overwritten.

So slight a monument to childhood may have given momentary encouragement to Jeff Logan of "The Crusader," who is in desperate search of his own past. Instinctively associating the emptiness and unaccountable sadness of his life with its lack of continuity, he returns to his home town in the San Joaquin Valley. But finding more signs of change than of permanence, he tries to distract himself by gambling in the marble game at the hotel cigar counter. The pin-ball machine is called "the crusader" by the manufacturer, and Saroyan uses it as a symbolic device to associate Jeff Logan's sense of loss with the problems of the American in general for whom the past has lost much of its meaning.[16] With no visible remains of a tradition, Jeff comes to believe that nothing has been lost. The pilgrimage of this modern knight ends in a pin-ball tournament in which the name of God is frequently and loudly invoked by the gamblers.

Using the technique of the omniscient author, Saroyan gives us all the thoughts of Jeff Logan, but he wisely denies him an awareness of his ironic conclusion. He also goes inside the minds of Joe, who runs the cigar counter and pin-ball machine, and of Mary Rusek, the Slavonian waitress who becomes conscious through Jeff of her spiritual need for some link with the past. Though this liberty of technique weakens both the unity and immediacy of the story, the obvious intensity of Saroyan's feeling and its pertinence to his more general subject of the immigrant and his children make it a valuable story.

The most important adult of *Little Children* is Sarkis of "Countryman, How Do You Like America?" Not only does his story serve as a basis for judging the distinction between the immigrants and their children but it also embodies the book's theme in a very special way. Sarkis comes to this country from Armenia in 1908 when he is not yet thirty. After a brief stay in the East, he finds his way to California where he gets a job in the vineyards, saves enough money for a down payment on a small acreage of his own, marries an Armenian girl, raises a family, sends his first son to high school, his second to college. He is proud and happy, but he can never overcome the deep dividedness within him. What emerges from this brief sketch is the nature of his emotional life which is balanced precariously between a joyous appreciation and an ineffable sadness that clings to him partly through temperamental heritage and partly through nostalgia for his homeland. Much of its power lies in the apparent artlessness of the story, but this effect was possible only because of the long, difficult period of work in which Saroyan learned to write with swiftness and ease. It would be an impertinence to object here that Saroyan had not rendered his scenes dramatically. Instead, he has given us a panoramic sweep of a man's life that is remarkable in such a brief story. Moreover, he has visualized his man and made tangible the valley in which he lived. What is perhaps an even greater achievement for the instinctively glib Saroyan, he has refrained from any intrusive comment. The story carries its own meaning.

The note of the comic is almost totally absent from the Fresno stories of the first books. It was with "The Ants" of *The Trouble with Tigers* that Saroyan began to cultivate the comedy of situation for its own sake.[17] Delightfully amusing, it exploits the amorality and aplomb of a penniless family. To make their incredible irresponsibilities convincing and to avoid any of the darker shadows implicit in the situation, Saroyan uses a young boy as narrator. Specifically, frankly, without anger or worry, he reports what he sees:

> We moved into a house once that the real estate man said was wonderful. What it had that was all right was a front porch Grandma could sit in a rocking chair on all day, which she began to do the day before we moved into the house, all eleven of us, counting Sam. Grandma liked the front porch so much she had me go seven blocks to our old house on Peachtree Street for her rocking chair and began sitting there the rest of the day.

By sunset the next day the family had carried in their things, "the water was running out of the kitchen faucet, the gas in the stove was heating stew, and the electricity was brightening the ten-cent mazda lamps from Woolworths." But the house was infested with ants. In the ensuing struggle the newcomers prove ineffectual in attack and ludicrous in defense, reducing themselves to undignified squirming and wiggling and flicking off the crawling ants. But they accept coexistence with an imperturbability possible only to those who never intend to pay their bills anyway. The narrator's sister is courted and won by a good-natured sailor who had never been to sea and had no money for a marriage license.

> It was truly a pleasant two months we spent in the new house, what with ants, the ship that John Tarhill stood on the deck of, and Velma's romance with him. After two months the different companies shut off the water and the gas and the lights and for a week we got along without them modern conveniences, but after a week the real estate man came and said we had to pay rent or get out and Grandma said, Pay rent? Why, boy, the house is full of ants. So that afternoon we moved to another house.

But "The Ants" provides the only comic relief of *The Trouble with Tigers*, and the mood sharply changes with the next story, "The Great Leapfrog Contest," which points up the essentially competitive nature of life in the valley for the children of immigrants. The contest is not an idle game but a test of endurance and determination which not only establishes a hierarchy among the children but also has implications for their future. "A Talk with Father" presents briefly but effectively the loneliness and awkwardness of a sixteen-year-old boy whose parents have separated. The fourth story in this series, "The Acrobats," renders its theme concretely and meaningfully without violating the point of view of a young girl who tells the story in language that is always simple but adequate. Its setting is a second-floor dental office from which the young narrator and her brother watch a troop of midgets perform in the street below. The meaning of the story emerges from the different reactions to the performance: some of the people are impatient with the intrusion, others are unaccountably afraid, still others are annoyed by the disturbance and wonder why the police do not interfere. And finally, of course, there is an adult who appreciates the picturesqueness of the performance and the human values implicit in the midgets' willingness to support themselves by what nature has given them.

The best of the sequence and one of the half-dozen best of

Saroyan is "Citizens of the Third Grade." The story is reflected through the intelligence of Miss Gavit, a teacher at the Cosmos Public School in the foreign section of the city. She is bewildered by the development of world events, especially by Mussolini's invasion of Abyssinia; she is particularly troubled by her boys in the third grade who reflect the animosities and tensions of these events. She keeps Tom Lucca after school to caution him against hurting the feelings of the Negro twins in the class. But she does not realize the degree of Tom's personal feelings, for she cannot see into his home life. Here Saroyan goes inside the mind of Tom Lucca, visualizes his home life and his absorption in his parent's conviction that the whole world is against the Italian. This shift in technique weakens the unity of the story, but increases its intensity by presenting racial loyalties more realistically than Miss Gavit could have done. The Negro twins, also sensitive about the invasion, view the news releases in terms of their own embattled position in the neighborhood. When the inevitable big fight comes, Miss Gavit is finally able to stop the fight, but she cannot get the boys to shake hands. Her feeling of helplessness before such deep-rooted problems is poignantly conveyed. Possibly no other story so effectively relates violence among nations to a sand-lot scrap. It is a story that has lost none of its effectiveness in the twenty-five years since it was written.

Several of the stories of *Peace, It's Wonderful* reflect the growing importance of the valley in Saroyan's writing. Three of them anticipate Saroyan's next book, *My Name is Aram*: one in theme, another in character portrayal, and a third in mood. A monologue, "1924 Cadillac For Sale," is spoken by a used-car salesman, an amused and philosophic observer of the human scene, who sees the "absurdity and beauty" of man's dedication to his automobile. "The Insurance Salesman, The Peasant, the Rug Merchant and the Potted Plant" is a parable on the incredible tenacity of insurance salesmen. Although amusing and colorful in its pictures of Arshag Gorobakian working among his own people of the San Joaquin Valley, it doesn't quite live up to the charm of its title. "The Warm, Quiet Valley of Home" reveals Saroyan's ability to combine sharpness of detail with an idyllic mood in writing of Fresno and the Valley. It begins vividly: "My cousin drove the broken-down Ford to the front of the house and pulled the emergency brake because the regular brakes were no good. The car skidded, choked and stopped." The two drive into the hills, drink a little beer, talk partly in Armenian and partly in English, fire salutes to their ancestors in the old country, and return to "the warm, quiet, lovely valley that was our home in the world."[18] A slight sketch, it nevertheless reveals Saroyan's love of home, his ability to convey a sense of place and at the same time keep us aware of the broader world beyond.

IV My Name is Aram

My Name is Aram (1940), the last of the series of short stories which have been traced in chapters one and two, is Saroyan's most serious bid for a single book that might prove representative of his achievement in short fiction. By this time he had evolved a style of swiftness and simplicity, an ability to select images both strikingly concrete and richly suggestive, and to create sharply visualized scenes without retarding the forward movement of his stories. It had been an arduous process of learning to know his most fruitful subject and to trust those techniques most natural to him. It may be surprising to speak of a new confidence in one whose brashness as a young writer was unrivaled, but the introduction to *Aram* contains a note of confidence that is quite different from the braggadocio and posturing of his earlier prefaces. He acknowledges his debts freely, not only to Edward Weeks and Edward J. O'Brien for their encouragement, but to Fresno for providing him with "an abundance of material by nature so rich in the elements of comedy as to require little or no labor to select and chronicle." Nothing in the book is entirely fiction, he says; no member of his family is fully there, but no one is fully absent. The ease and sincerity of these tributes imply the strength of his realization that, although the people of *Aram* sprang from his remembered past, they bore the uniqueness of *his* imagination and temperament and possessed their life and meaning only because he had worked out an adequate technique for turning the facts of personal history into the truths of fiction. "All humanity" is in the "proud and angry Saroyans," he says, and one can see "the large comic world" in the little city of Fresno.[19]

In writing of children Saroyan placed himself in an old and prominent tradition of American literature. There are ideological moorings for *Aram* in Ralph Waldo Emerson, who expressed a philosophical respect for childhood by assuring authors that a little girl or a "couple of school-boys" could bring them closer to truth than could the epic subjects of the world. The American Transcendentalists agreed with William Wordsworth that the child is closer to nature and therefore to God than is man. Though later in the nineteenth century the bad boy became popular in fiction, it was a temporary countermovement within the family rather than a new strain. The bad boy was not really bad; he was just an irritant to a society that had become overly concerned with respectability. There has never been an American line of descent from Lazarillo de Tormes or Moll Flanders or other young people of European literature whose aim was to learn the rules of an adult world, no matter how corrupt, so that they could adapt to its ways and prosper. Instead, American writers have emphasized the shock and recoil of the young in their first awareness of evil. From Nathaniel Hawthorne, Henry James, Stephen Crane, and Mark Twain, to Ernest Hemingway, Carson McCullers, and J. D. Salinger, American writers have postulated a division between youth and age and have generally assumed the essential goodness of children and their superiority and incorruptibility because of this innocence. Huck Finn escaped corruption and finally withdrew beyond the domesticating reach of society. The pain of initiation left Nick Adams scarred, Holden Caulfield emotionally disturbed, and Frankie Addams permanently aware of her essential aloneness. But who would doubt their continued decency?[20]

What sets Saroyan apart from the mainline of this tradition, contrary to popular assumptions, is not the innocence of his children or their apparent immunity to evil. The difference relates to the conflicts in his stories, which do not derive from adult-child polarities but from contradictory impulses within the heart of man. Saroyan was aware of Mark Twain's great achievement in presenting society through the eyes of a boy, for *Huckleberry Finn* was one of his favorite books; and some of Saroyan's earlier stories, such as "The War" and "The Oranges" turn on the child's resentment of the indifference, inadequacy, and cruelty of adults. In turning away from this obviously fertile field, however, he was instinctively following a tack more suitable to his qualities of mind and more intimately a part of his own experience. *Little Children,* as I have pointed out, presents the immigrant and his children in the difficult process of becoming Americanized; but its social criticism, though valid and significant, is only a by-product of the author's unerring sense of the way things were. This was life in the valley, he is saying; I am sharing it honestly; see what it means.

With *My Name is Aram* Saroyan became more conscious of an age-old, universal aspect of the subject before his eyes: the conflicting claims of dream and reality had a very personal meaning for people who had severed ties with home and country to come half-way around the world in search of a new life. They had found that the "Golden West" was not an eldorado or a paradise but simply a place to live, good enough if they worked hard. Moreover, enough time had passed for them to achieve some tranquility and resignation in weighing the validity of hope against the constant pull of disappointment. In such an environment the poetic and the practical seemed to have genealogies of their own and were visible in distinct personalities. It required time and the perspective of distance for Saroyan to understand this spirit of his people and to know that it would provide him with more than a point of view: it would become his truest subject. To read his books in sequence from *The Daring Young Man on the Flying Trapeze* to *My Name is Aram* is to see how gradually but inevitably Saroyan found his way into this subject.

Thus *My Name is Aram* is not essentially about childhood. It seeks out instances of poetic involvement and develops them in relationship to the claims of the practical. Recognizing no essential difference between youth and age, it presents many adults who are forever childlike and some children who are never young. The narrator is an adult recalling his youth, and Aram is therefore both man and boy. To the extent that the pronoun of the book's title has a precise meaning, it refers to a residue of romantic responsiveness from the narrator's youth. In this sense the child is father to the man, a Wordsworthian dictum which, if it can be used outside the context of platonic idealism, means an awareness of continuity that strengthens the narrator's impression of self, not as subject but as reflector. (For the book is less about Aram than about other Garoghlanians, especially uncles, who make up the most memorable portraits.) Saroyan's feeling for life quickened as he turned back to the time and place of his boyhood.

Since Aram's actions and thoughts are recollected, the book sacrifices much of the suspense and vividness possible to contemporaneous reporting. It should not be judged finally in terms of conflict, though most of its stories have a dramatic structure and all of them place a poetic sensitivity in some kind of opposition to the demands of practicality. But Aram is never really involved in conflict; he learns nothing about himself or about his associates through a course of action: the recognition belongs to the mature mind in retrospect and inheres in its mood of nostalgia. The value of the book lies in the quality of its lyricism, where it should finally be judged. Though its lyricism cannot produce the vitality and sustaining force of dramatic tension, it does illuminate the more accessible pleasures of daily living. The book gives this kind of pleasure. And to its great credit, the mood of nostalgia, though indispensable to the speaker, does not transfer itself to the reader. Instead, the book evokes a feeling for the preciousness of the moment and a recognition of a continuing capacity for responsiveness such as one could never have known as a child. Thus the book escapes sentimentality, not through its comic strain, as is widely believed, but through the casual and unobtrusive way in which its major theme gives body and form to the individual stories and to the book as a whole. Though not profound or complex, it is an intellectually respectable theme, and in *Aram* Saroyan has made it appear inseparable from its subject and from the technique of retrospect.

The stories of *Aram* fall into two groups: in those like "The Summer of the Beautiful White Horse," "The Journey to Hanford," "The Circus," and "A Word to Scoffers," the rival claims of the poetic and the practical are harmoniously resolved; but "Pomegranate Trees," "The Fifty-Yard Dash," "My Cousin Dikran, the Orator," "The Three Swimmers and the Grocer from Yale," and "The Poor and Burning Arab," stories that emphasize man's inability to realize his dreams, suggest some kind of permanent opposition that is a necessary condition of human existence. The first group dominates the tone of Aram, primarily because of the advantageous position of its stories; but the second provides an important balance which prevents the book from falling into a facile, unconvincing optimism.

By far the best of the first group are "The Summer of the Beautiful White Horse," which opens the book, and "The Journey to Hanford," which immediately follows. In the one, Aram and his cousin Mourad take a horse from their neighbor's barn, stable it secretly at an abandoned farm, and treat themselves to early morning rides. Of course they admit no intention of stealing, for the Garoghlanians have a strong family tradition of honesty. And, when they finally return the horse, it is stronger and better spirited than ever. The story is well insulated against any shock of detection or punishment, for everyone is on the same side. When Uncle Khosrove is informed by the owner, a gentle Assyrian named John Byro, that the horse is missing, he drowns out the man's laments by shouting in a loud voice: "It's no harm. What is the loss of a horse? Haven't we all lost the homeland? What is this crying over a horse?" And when the owner comes upon the boys one morning, he slyly pretends not to recognize the horse they are riding, a gesture made plausible by his realization that the surprise encounter will in itself frighten the boys into returning his property and, even more, by his noting the obvious improvement in his horse.

The softening effects of memory are appropriate to this story, particularly since it retains vitality through the humor of the adults, through such incidental touches as the inadequacy of Aram as rider, and, above all, through the colorful picture of two small boys leaping vineyards at daybreak on a beautiful white horse.

In the other, "The Journey to Hanford," Aram's grandmother manages to preserve a precarious harmony between her brusque husband and her impractical, music-loving son. Aram and his Uncle Jorgi are given food and rent money for one month and sent to the neighboring village of Hanford where Aram is expected to cook and keep house while his uncle is to earn money harvesting watermelons. But Jorgi spends the time idly strumming his zither and returns broke. The grandmother, however, spares the family any angry reckoning by bringing forth money of her own which she allows her husband to assume is Jorgi's. The old woman lifts her long skirts, takes the currency from a pocket in her undergarments, and gives it to Aram: "When his father comes home, give him this money." She looks at the boy a moment, speaks his name quietly, and says nothing more. But it is a stratagem which implies clearly her realization that, when balance cannot be achieved by the individual, it must be supplied by the family; and her wisdom is justified by the closing picture of her husband listening contentedly to the singing and playing of Jorgi. The family could no more dispense with Jorgi's music than with her own shrewd management. "When you read in a book that a father loves a foolish son more than his wise sons," the father mutters dreamily, "that writer is a bachelor."[21]

The two opening stories make their points unpretentiously, with economy of words and with complete trust in the story elements to convey their own meanings, and they derive a particular charm from the wry grin of the author. In the same vein but less successful are such stories as "The Circus," in which two boys receive token punishment for absenting themselves from school; "Locomotive 38, the Ojibway," in which Aram serves as zealous though inexpert chauffeur to a wealthy, eccentric Indian; and "Old Country Advice to the American Traveler," which is little more than a thumbnail lecture on the importance of trust but one which handles its subject in an amusing, anecdotal manner.

This group receives a kind of rhetorical period from the concluding story, "A Word to Scoffers." An editorial piece thinly disguised as fiction, it is an unfortunate retrogression of the author to an earlier habit and it weakens *Aram* seriously: It destroys the unifying effect of the valley setting by taking the reader to Reno and Salt Lake City; it is marred by an incidental and irrelevant preachiness, as when the narrator denounces gambling. It turns on an incident in which Aram is supposedly converted to a life of faith by a tall, melancholy follower of Brigham Young; but there is really no conversion since Aram has always been in essential agreement with the stranger's message. Moreover, the lesson of faith, more pointedly and convincingly advanced in preceding stories, has now become impossibly diluted: one must believe in everything.

But the greatest disservice of the closing piece lies in the framework which it seems to provide, combining with the first story to establish its indiscriminate optimism as a kind of fundamental reference for the entire book. Fortunately, however, all the stories of *Aram* cannot be forced into this framework. Indeed, those that resist are as a group the best of the book and are primarily responsible for its effectiveness as a whole. Stories like "The Summer of the Beautiful White Horse" and "The Journey to Hanford," valuable in themselves, gain strength from their association with the contrasting group; for it is in such stories as "Pomegranate Trees" and "The Poor and Burning Arab" that Saroyan's affirmation is placed against an unflinching recognition of forces that deny.

In these stories Aram is not a participant but an observer. For the most part they are told so simply that they seem to have no technique at all. But Aram is an ideal reporter. He has a sharp eye for detail and a noncommittal manner characteristic of a boy but suggestive of greater meanings than a boy could plausibly perceive. In "Pomegranate Trees" he tells of Uncle Melik who tries determinedly and imaginatively to turn a barren tract of land into a beautiful orchard. Melik spares neither time nor money but inevitably his dreams of a garden paradise is defeated by the dryness and heat of the desert, and he stands by helplessly as his land reverts to the irrepressible cactus and horned toad. In this story Aram's instinctive scepticism provides an important ballast, yet he has a boyish sense of the grandeur of his uncle's struggle.

In another story Aram tells of Uncle Gyko who reads Oriental philosophy and fasts according to Eastern asceticism. Gyko grows hollow-cheeked but never finds the mysterious forces within him. His failure is paralleled by Aram's own disappointment. The boy coaxes enough money from his reluctant uncle to suscribe in part to a correspondence course in body building and self-development. As a test of his new prowess, he enters athletic contests at school. In the climactic fifty-yard dash, however, he discovers that no amount of faith in his own powers enables him to overtake the swifter runners ahead.

In telling about his cousin Dikran, Aram says more than he realizes about how elaborately society rationalizes its failure to keep peace in the world. It thus reminds us of the voice of the man in recollection while it manages to retain the boyishness of the report itself. Dikran, the only serious student in the family, prepares a formal oration in which he drew upon learned and brilliant books to prove that those who were killed in World War I did not die in vain. His grandfather is both proud and disturbed. It is a large and beautiful thesis, he tells Dikran, one that he will accept from a boy but not from a man. Its deeply felt pacifism may have seemed a little dated to readers of the 1950's but with renewed hopes for test-ban treaties it once again seems timely. But the value of "My Cousin Dikran, the Orator" lies primarily in its vital pictures of the Armenian farmers who gather in church basements to listen to speeches. To them oratory is more than a means of expression; it is a much-needed personal release. The family whose son could deliver an oration was proud indeed. If a visiting orator made a plea for funds, individuals would rise from the audience and pledge money with solemn pride in their carefully chosen words and manner of delivery: "Gone are the days of poverty for this tribe from the lovely city of Dikranagert," one would say, and the applause had less to do with the amount of his pledge than with his dramatic pronunciation of the old-world names of his children in whose names he was donating.[22] These vivid pictures, reminding one of the vogue of oratory which helped form the literary fashions elsewhere in America, convey a love of words which no doubt influenced Saroyan's literary ambitions as much as did his afternoons at the public library.

In "The Three Swimmers and the Grocer from Yale," mud and rain are too much for a group of young boys who swim naked in Thompson's Ditch. They repeatedly assure themselves, however, that they "sure showed that river," but they are in retreat. A grocer in a nearby store gives them more food and drink than their money can buy. He is one of them in spirit, and is himself in retreat before implacable forces of another kind. He is soon replaced in the store by a prudent fellow who tidies up and insists on cash. The boys had liked this grocer, though they never realized that he was one of them in spirit. They finally conclude that he must have been crazy, a conclusion that extends by implication to any person who too stubbornly disregards the demands of prudence and practicality. The story suffers from a mannered, rather obvious comic device of the grocer's talk that is supposed to be colorful in the way of legendary old-timers. Moreover, the purpose of his college education is left ambiguous and keeps the story off balance, but the story makes its point and does so by the implications of its action.

All the force of this mysterious incapacity of man to fulfill himself is concentrated in "The Poor and Burning Arab," not a story but a portrait of an immigrant who knew no English and only a little Armenian. Starved for companionship, the Arab clings to his friendship with Aram's Uncle Khosrove. Their relationship is compounded of humor and sadness, the humor relating primarily to the explosive Khosrove who keeps silent company with the lonely Arab. Perspective is gained through the device of a narrator whose youth encourages the reader to perceive what the boy himself is too young to understand. An effective juxtaposing of story elements is gained by the boy's paging through the *Saturday Evening Post* in the room adjacent to the men, looking at ads for jello, for ready-made clothes, automobiles, and other signs of sophistication in a society changing too rapidly for many of its old-world figures. The sketch is visualized without elaboration.

CHAPTER 4

The Time of His Life

SAROYAN'S STYLE steadily improved throughout the sequence of books which began with *The Daring Young Man* (1934) and concluded with *My Name is Aram* (1940). During this period of prolific effort—by his own estimate he wrote more than five hundred tales in these years—he learned to get into his story immediately; to fit character, setting, and mood to the action; to express with colloquial vigor what his people were capable of saying, and to imply much about what they were able to feel. His style grew lean, partly because of the influence of Hemingway and partly because of his own reaction to the criticism that he tended to talk too much. In establishing setting, he began to dispense with description altogether and to rely on simple statement: a bar on Third Avenue, a lunch counter on Kearney Street, or a frame house in Fresno. Ignoring appearances and backgrounds of his characters, he began to do little more than assign names to his people and to start them talking. Because of his mastery of colloquial speech, these sketches often appeared vital and significant when they were at times no more than incomplete exercises in dramatic composition. But, at their best, they achieved moments of genuine recognition; and at such times the economy of drama became an important virtue of his story form.

With the appearance of *Little Children*, midway through this period of short fiction, it became evident that Fresno would replace San Francisco as his favorite setting and that childhood would become more important than young manhood as a focal point. Many of his readers regarded this change as a sign of weakness. In an age highly conscious of ideological uses of literature, it was perhaps understandable that his turning back to childhood would be considered a retreat from responsibility. As we get farther from the period, however, and view Saroyan's work in a larger perspective, it becomes apparent that this movement was not a retreat but a growth.

For one thing, the change was inevitable and a largely unconscious adjustment to the essential Romanticism of his outlook. For, although Saroyan had been Naturalistic in subject, he had not adopted the Naturalist's attitudes. The typical young man of his early fiction was a kind of Wordsworthian innocent; his goodness of heart was axiomatic. Though he frequented bars and gambling rooms and struggled to maintain himself in an intensely competitive depression-ridden city, he remained uncorrupted. Saroyan had not wished to explore the effect of environment on character. The people he had known most intimately from his childhood days seemed insulated from their surroundings by a separate language and by customs and convictions brought from the land of their birth. Thus, in respect to moral character, Saroyan instinctively assumed a superiority of heritage over environment, an assumption that reflected, too, his own indomitable sense of self. It was his intimate knowledge of the immigrants of the San Joaquin Valley that shaped his view of the people whom he encountered in San Francisco.

Indeed, the cosmopolitan flavor of the city no doubt encouraged him to regard it—at least in the attitudes of those existing on the fringes of society there—as a kind of extended Fresno. He perceived the loneliness and uncertainty beneath their reserve and brusqueness. He assumed that, like the people he had known best, they accepted alienation as an unavoidable condition of life and thus in the deepest sense were impervious to place. In his fiction these people were in the city but not of the city; they were drifters who no longer belonged in any one place. In turning to Fresno, Saroyan simply put them back into the setting where he had first come to know them, which is to say that he was moving closer to the springs of his own creativity.

Insofar as the problems of modern man relate most characteristically to urban, industrial situations, Saroyan was of course turning away from subjects and themes that seemed most central to his age. But any basic conflict between man and his environment would have been unlikely in Saroyan's writing because of his assumption of the inviolability of the individual. There would have been no real contest. The determinists of the time were loading the scales against the individual; but Saroyan would have loaded it in his favor. Granting Saroyan's optimistic view of human nature, it was fortunate indeed that he followed where his inclinations led—to the rural and small-town environment, a setting always more congenial to Romanticism.

But the Fresno setting has another important relationship to Saroyan's growth as artist. The young people in his fiction of the city were, for the most part, projections of his own personality; when they were not, they tended to be unconvincing and uninteresting. Paradoxically, to get away from the omnipresence of self, Saroyan had to return to his childhood. In recalling persons whom he had known in his most formative years, he was able to get beyond the confines of his own personality. In this process of recollection he could grow unmindful of self even as he felt most genuinely himself. In this instance he was rarely, if ever, imitative of other writers. He was marvelously free of self-consciousness and awkwardness, as is so clearly demonstrated in both style and subject. *Little Children* and *My Name is Aram* are not about Saroyan's childhood, nor really about childhood at all. They are about the immigrants of Fresno and the San Joaquin Valley, the people recalled from his boyhood days whose images gave him the impetus to extend himself beyond the lyricism of his early tales to the more dramatic later ones. The uncles, cousins, and neighbors of Aram, while containing enough of the author to possess vitality and immediacy, are distinct in themselves. If Saroyan had not discovered the literary uses of Fresno and the valley, he could not have given us the best of his short stories—nor his plays.

I My Heart's in the Highlands

In this respect, it is helpful to consider the genesis of his first successful play, *My Heart's in the Highlands.* Appearing originally as a short story in *Three Times Three* (1926), it was reshaped the following year for William Kozlenko's *One-Act Play Magazine,* reprinted by Scribner's in *Contemporary One-Act Plays*

(1938), and finally expanded in 1939 into a near full-length play for the Broadway production of the Group Theatre.[1] As a short story its form was that of an episode recalled from early childhood. Its narrator was still young, presumably, for his language and manner of presentation had not lost their boyishness or spontaneity. Yet he was mature enough to recognize the integrity and indelibility of his earlier experience. Thus there was no hesitation or uncertainty in the telling. Like the best of Saroyan's tales, it combined a tone of wide-eyed freshness with the sureness of hindsight.

Because this story remained substantially unchanged in both dramatic versions, it merits recounting briefly: a young boy, whose name is Johnny, lives on San Benito Avenue in Fresno with his grandmother and his father, an unpublished poet. One day an old man ambles down the street playing a bugle, stops in front of the house, finishes his song, and asks for a drink of water. When he has drained an entire pitcher of cool water in one long draught, he introduces himself as Jasper MacGregor, an actor, and suggests that a little bread and cheese would lighten his spirits. The famliy is without food or money, but Johnny is sent to the corner store to wheedle credit for a loaf of bread and a pound of cheese. The snack only taunts their appetites, but at Johnny's insistence the old man takes up his bugle once more and plays with such plaintive beauty that neighbors gather, bringing gifts of food: eggs, potatoes, sausage, or whatever they can spare from their cupboards. The old man stays on with the family, living in a kind of pastoral simplicity, until after seventeen days an officer of the Old People's Home comes for him, saying that he must return to help them in their annual show.

The story is essentially dramatic. It is strongly visualized, though it has almost no description. Faithful to the language and horizons of its youthful narrator, its conversations are remembered in direct, monosyllabic simplicity. The element of fantasy is balanced by the boy's realistic grasp of poverty and made plausible by the personality and character of the old man himself. Jasper MacGregor is a poseur, harmless and genial, but self-interested. Yet there is unearthly longing in his heart; and, because he is able to communicate this longing through the soul-stirring music of his bugle, he brings about a miraculous multiplying of loaves and fishes. Suggesting meanings far beyond itself, the story thus achieves a parable-like power.

But it suffers from incredible haste in composition and might well have remained buried in Saroyan's least-successful book had not William Kozlenko, the editor of *One-Act Play Magazine*, suggested that Saroyan adapt it for the stage. With very few changes the author got it ready for the December, 1937, issue of Kozlenko's journal. He eliminated the device of recollection, relieved Johnny of the narrator's function, but left the dialogue virtually unchanged. Although the setting was only implied in the story, it became more significant in the play. Stage directions emphasized the poverty and initial isolation of the family: their house, a broken-down frame structure with large front porch, is situated on bleak land somewhat apart from neighboring houses, and the outside world is represented only by a distant train whistle and a passing newsboy.

Although the changes were few, the dramatic form opened new possibilities for the growth of the original idea. The characters themselves, set free from the memory and fancy of a narrator, gained a chance to live in their own right. The old man, vividly imagined in the story, needed little modification and responded well to the transfer. His hunger and thirst seemed even more real when supported by whimsical and emphatic stage gestures. Yet this hunger and thirst were not theatrical only, for attesting to a parallel spiritual longing they were genuinely dramatic. The more substantial Jasper MacGregor became as a person the more convincing were the ineffable implications of his music. And in the play both were directly measurable through their impact on others. As for the neighbors, this impact was presented through a kind of simplified religious pageant—a communal testimony to man's spiritual banishment and to his desire to recover a lost sense of fellowship in a ritual-like sharing of bread and song.

Jasper MacGregor was so fully realized in the imagination of Saroyan that even a partial projection of his person implied the whole. From the first, he needed no further development. But insofar as his dramatic value consisted of his impact on others—and the symbol of the bugle implies a good deal about the author's intention here—the play failed to fulfill its own terms.

This failure relates especially to Johnny's father. His attitudes and motivations, though not of first importance when he existed only in his son's memory, as he did in the story, had to take on a life of his own when transferred to the play. More specifically, he had to react significantly and convincingly to the old man. But Saroyan did not give him this identity. (It is notable that in the play, as in the story, he is left nameless.) His initial reaction to Jasper MacGregor was measurable, of course; but, after the departure of the old man, there was no indication of any genuine, enduring effect.

For the first time in his career, however, Saroyan overcame his unwillingness to rework material. Characteristically, he did no rewriting; instead he extended the play, adding what was really a long second act. In this instance, his reluctance to rewrite proved helpful; for, in preserving the first part intact, he avoided the risk of losing the evanescent charm of the original. At the same time, he insured the unity of the larger play by giving over the expanded portion primarily to explication and restatement. Such obvious indifference to customary dramatic structure brought objections from many of the critics. Some charged him with padding his material, others with abandoning all form. Despite these objections, the new play possessed an inner coherence; and it enlarged significantly the meaning of the original.

This effect was achieved primarily through the character development of Johnny's father, Ben Alexander, whose poetry, because of the recent death of his wife, expresses themes of loss and remembrance. Though not specifically mentioned in the first play, or what is really act one of the second, her death was a plausible inference, accounting not only for Johnny's eager questions concerning the whereabouts of Jasper MacGregor's mother but also for Ben's withdrawal. Up to the opening of the extended portion, Ben's actions have not handicapped the family seriously. He has kept a roof over their heads, and their poverty has been remarkably untroubled. Moreover, however naïvely, Ben has been awaiting an acceptance check from *The Atlantic Monthly* which he believes will solve their financial problems and justify his life as poet. But three months have passed since the departure of Jasper MacGregor, and the consequences of Ben's refusal to earn his bread have become grim. The family faces eviction and Johnny has begun to steal from nearby vineyards.

The climax comes swiftly and simultaneously for both father and son, involving each in his own way. For Ben, it begins with a rejection slip. And later the same day Johnny, returning from a vineyard, has been chased home by a mongrel dog barking at his heels. The dog is harmless, but the boy, uneasy in conscience, sees it as a watchdog and thinks the master is in pursuit. Ben tries to laugh away his son's terror; but, when footsteps are heard on the porch, Ben too is overcome by fear. With the help of the grandmother, they barricade the front door with their flimsy furniture, piling on their few belongings in comic-pathetic desperation. The pounding at the door turns out to be not that of a policeman or an angry farmer, however, but that of Jasper MacGregor, who must sound his bugle to break the siege.

Once again neighbors, bringing food, gather around the old man. But he is too weak to play more than a few strains on his bugle, and when the officer comes from the Old People's Home, he is dead. Ben and Johnny and the grandmother put a few belongings into a small bag and leave the house. Their furniture, Ben says, will pay the back rent. As they go out, Ben tries to comfort his son and to assure him that everything will be all right.

Thus the climax is at once humorous and pathetic. The prospect of the old woman, the poet, and the boy barricading themselves in their flimsy fortress, with nothing to fear from the world but themselves, is a fine touch. Through his many short stories Saroyan had developed this talent for the small subject, but nowhere has he achieved more humor, warmth, and pathos through an incidental effect. Though the climax is conceived in that serio-comic vein which can so easily slip into sentimentality, his people are alive and believable. In a very real sense Ben Alexander is rescued by Jasper MacGregor. Fortunately, Saroyan does not attempt to articulate what Ben has learned from the old man. Instead, he allows character to reveal itself through action, and the meaning to emerge through the impact of one character upon another. Moreover, emotional balance is maintained by the earthy scepticism of the boy, who says in the closing lines: "I'm not mentioning any names, Pa, but something's wrong someplace."

It has never been easy for American playwrights to catch the tone of mingled sadness and joy. Our plays are all anger or frustration, all cynicism, all tragedy, or all comedy. From the opening lines of this play, however, when Johnny wonders what highlands the old man is talking about until his final sceptical rejoinder, there is a spirit of humor that plays through the lines. It is not a humor of witty lines, and it is rarely brought in for its own sake. Deriving from a sympathetic awareness of man's inadequacies, it is often wistful, as when Ben Alexander attempts to pay his grocery bill with a sheaf of unpublished poems, or when Johnny awakens his father to ask how he is feeling.

There is little point in quarreling with the play's structure, for its value lies in its circular form and in its juxtaposition of moods. Without breaking the spell of fantasy, Saroyan managed to project the theme along four levels of human experience: realism in the boy, defiance in the father, resignation in the grandmother, and mysticism in the old man. Nor is there any point in criticizing the play for its vagueness. The longing in the heart of man is always vague. It is enough that Saroyan has given us a vividly imagined people who reflect this longing convincingly. Whereas the short story had been named "The Man with his Heart in the Highlands," the play is called "My Heart's in the Highlands," bringing it closer to the poem of Robert Burns from which the idea derives and suggesting a more generalized meaning: the uprootedness of the immigrant presented in terms of the universal theme of spiritual exile.

The play opened at the Guild Theatre in New York, April 13, 1939. Though scheduled for only five performances as part of the Group Theatre's experimental program, favorable press notices enabled it to run for six weeks. In general, those who objected to the play asked for more ordered thought, more specific symbols, and for plot. Had it developed the social protest or the plight of the artist which are implicit in the first version, the play would have won wider support. Yet its defenders far outnumbered its attackers. George Jean Nathan, Richard Watts, Brooks Atkinson, Otis Ferguson, John Mason Brown, and others welcomed it as a moving and thoroughly enjoyable departure from the usual fare served up by the theater of the time.[2]

II *Commedia dell'Arte*

My Heart's in the Highlands was not Saroyan's first dramatic venture. In May, 1935, while waiting to embark for Europe, he saw an item in the New York *Times* which reported that he was at work on a play. In order to save the paper from lying, as he put it, he devoted his remaining five days to writing a play. No producer in New York wanted *Subway Circus,* as he entitled it, and the following year his youthful board of directors in Los Angeles excluded the play from *Three Times Three.* Saroyan, uncharacteristically modest about this work, confessed that it was probably not worth the financial risk of producing.

Nevertheless *Subway Circus* tells us more about Saroyan's original notion of the theater than do his direct pronouncements on the subject, and this knowledge helps to keep his later plays in perspective. Its basic scene is the inside of a subway train, and the background noises throughout are those of a train moving at different speeds or stopping at stations to pick up and discharge passengers. Despite an impersonal, unselective grouping of people, its focus is primarily on the individual, dramatizing in ten sequences the dream visions of individual passengers. As the spotlight picks out one person, the subway car divides in the middle, and the setting of that person's dream world comes into view. The theme that holds these sequences together is the contrast between dream and reality: a cripple sees himself as an acrobat; a schoolboy examines his teacher; a timid, inarticulate clerk declares love eloquently to a secretary in his office. "Here is the world of one man at a time," Saroyan says, "the inner, the boundless, the ungeographic world of wakeful dreams." In juxtaposing unlikely elements he sometimes achieves a startling, surrealistic effect: a sandwich man thinks he is God; a Salvation-Army Sergeant sees himself preaching hell-fire to a drunk, a Marxist student, and a whore only to discover to his own horror that it is he who fears death.

Some of the sequences are only sketched in and consist more of stage directions than dialogue. But it was not haste alone that caused the script to be thus incomplete. Saroyan obviously regarded the theater as a cooperative enterprise in which everyone from director to errand boy collaborated in working out the playwright's initial idea. *Subway Circus* was intended as a kind of latter-day *commedia dell'arte,* less as a script than a series of proposals for theatrical development. It would have required highly imaginative improvisers to perform. Saroyan seemed to think of a play as less a matter of discourse than of miming or showing in the ancient sense, suggesting in some ways the theater of Thornton Wilder or of Jacques Copeau and André Obey, whose work was coming to the attention of Americans during the mid-1930's.[3] It seems that in America only one so far from the center of things—so temperamentally as well as geographically outside the world of the Broadway theater—could have approached the modern stage in this anachronistic way.

This sense of the pageantry of drama is what ties together most of Saroyan's plays. It was such a fundamental departure from the main conventions of the modern drama—from the theater of ideas that has come down to us from Ibsen and Shaw—that, when Saroyan's two most remarkable plays appeared, *My Heart's in the Highlands* and *The Time of Your Life,* critics had difficulty classifying them. They were called "experimental," a cautious catch-all term that had validity in respect to the Group Theatre's production of the first of these but not to the play itself or to *The Time of Your Life.* They were also referred to as fantasies, and their symbolism and surrealism noted. But no one thought of these tags as adequate or as even convincing. In my opinion, these plays cannot be understood apart from Saroyan's fiction, not only in what the latter tells us generally about the shaping of his imagination but more specifically in what it makes clear about the origins of his sense of theatrical form. His early stories, particularly those of *Inhale and Exhale,* indicate that "the world of the theatre," as he entitled one of his sketches, was almost as much a daily part of his life as being a newsboy in Fresno. To save his hard-earned dimes, he exchanged newspapers for tickets, or if possible slipped undetected by the doorman. One way or another, he saw all the movies and most of the vaudeville in town. Thus the world of his theater was fashioned for him by the movies of decades from 1910 through the 1920's and most especially by the Keith, Pantages, and Orpheum circuits. This initial experience with the theater was to leave its mark on his most characteristic drama.[4]

What sets his work off from that of other playwrights of the late 1930's was not its element of fantasy. Thornton Wilder's *Our Town* had appeared in the spring of 1938 and Maxwell Anderson's *The Star Wagon* in the previous year, both plays aiming at lyric rather than dramatic effects. Paradoxically, it was one of America's most indigenous art forms, the vaudeville, reincarnating itself in Saroyan's plays that made them appear so out of place on the American stage. Saroyan wanted no imaginary fourth wall to separate his players from the audience; instead, he sometimes asked them to talk directly to the audience, or go into dance routines, or do instrumental solos. He used the walk-on drunk, the comic monologue, oddities such as toys and guns as focal points for gags and topical references. His most characteristic unit was the incident, suggestive in itself but not readily extended into plot. And his characters, for the most part, were devised for the situation, often sketched in to illustrate an aspect of a general theme and identified only by such simple designations as an old man, a poet, a Negro, a hoofer. This is the stuff of vaudeville. And the very looseness of form suited well the improvisatory method of writing which Saroyan had cultivated through his short fiction.

Through this *potpourri* he expressed his sense of life as he found it in Fresno and San Francisco, not only in the attitudes and manners of the common people, the flavor of whose small talk he had learned to catch—sometimes to caricature—in simple, representative ways, but more importantly in the passions of the heart, especially of the immigrant Americans. He was willing to talk about these general passions of the heart without fear of sentimentality. The success of his characterization lies in the fact that, though his people are not complex, not developed in and for themselves. It is this representative quality that conceals their essential flatness. In the Scotsman of *My Heart's in the Highlands,* for example, Saroyan reflected the loneliness and uprootedness of the foreign-born American, regardless of national origin. He knew and understood those whose hearts were five thousand miles away. In the long series of stories beginning with "Seventy-

Thousand Assyrians" Saroyan had learned to re-create this character imaginatively. It is he more than "the daring young man" who is Saroyan's truly inimitable creation, his most valuable contribution to our literature.

This foreign-born American is also mixed with more native types. Jasper MacGregor incorporates into himself something of the itinerant slicker of our folk literature. He is the amiable fake who can talk his way into free meals and lodging, a type invariably associated in our folk imagination with the Yankee peddler. (Notice that Jasper MacGregor says his grandmother is in White River, Vermont, though her heart, too, is in the highlands five thousand miles away.) Looking carefully at Jasper MacGregor in Saroyan's first successful play, we need not be surprised that within a short time he would use a traveling vendor of patent medicines as a protagonist, as he does in *Love's Old Sweet Song.*

III The Time of Your Life

The Time of Your Life is the best of Saroyan's plays because it expresses most completely his mind and art. In form it consists largely of incidental routines: a hoofer, played originally by Gene Kelly, dances and does comic monologues; a Negro improvises mood pieces on the piano; an Arab pours his sadness into the harmonica; a crusty old-timer tells tall tales of the early West. There are such miscellaneous items as a gum-chewing contest and a Salvation Army band, while in the background a young man struggles continuously with a pinball machine. The scene is water-front honky-tonk in San Francisco, "an American place," says the stage directions, and yet its cosmopolitan flavor is apparent. The proprietor is Nick, of Italian birth. At the bar is the silent Arab, with a Mohammedan tattoo on his left hand to indicate that he has been to Mecca. A Greek newsboy sings Irish songs. At the piano is Wesley, a Negro whose music, like that of the Arab, evokes a sense of suffering from long ago and far away. The native American environment, both past and present, is represented, too—the past as it is mythologized in the popular imagination; the present as reflected in economic, social, and moral conflicts.

An effective combining of past and present is achieved in

Kitty Duval, who tells of her youth in a small Ohio town. She remembers the large house, the shade trees, and the big dog asleep on the doormat. But Kitty is a streetwalker, not a standard on-stage prostitute but one with such indubitable goodness of heart that one might think of her as a descendent of the bosomy, whisky-voiced habitué of the Western saloon, a type that has grown more pensive and fragile with the years. She reminds us of a world behind swinging doors in which the tart had status and even a kind of legal immunity. But earlier days are more specifically recalled by a crusty swaggerer who introduces himself as "an old trapper." Kit Carson, as he is called at Nick's, provides some lively comic interludes and turns out to be indispensable to the main drift of the play. He comes in asking a patron if he had ever fallen in love with a midget weighing thirty-nine pounds, and then Kit unlooses a glib, breezy string of anecdotes. In New Mexico, he had bashed in a man's head with a brass cuspidor; in Texas, he had fought with a six-footer whose right hand was an iron claw; in Toledo, he had herded cattle on a bicycle: "Easiest thing in the world. Rode no hands. Had to, otherwise couldn't lasso the cows." Caught cheating in a poker game, he had been saved by a tornado—he was sure of it, for he remembered "sitting on the roof of a two-story house, floating northwest."

Kit Carson tells these yarns to Joe, a wistful, quiet-mannered fellow who regards Nick's place as a kind of microcosm and spends his waking hours sipping champagne.[5] Joe is the first man ever to believe these stories. "Of course I believe you," Joe assures him. "Living is an art. It's not bookkeeping. It takes a lot of rehearsing for a man to get to be himself." Joe needs this mythologizing imagination, for it builds up an America he wants to know and accept. In this and in other ways, he is representative of his generation. He has come out of the depression having devised an economic system that goes on making money for him even as he has begun to see some of its less desirable consequences. In reaction against the vast impersonality of the new economics, he is no longer impressed by money alone and considers himself lucky not to know personally all those who have been hurt by his own rise to wealth. He now lives by a Christian conscience, he says, not by a social one. Hence he has a new-found respect for the little man and realizes that well-meaning people can make messes of their lives. He has saved the life of his dull but devoted *Johannes fac totum,* Tom, and he is eager to dispense kindness and charity wherever possible.

Joe provides the central reference point of the play, but the play is not about Joe, or about any other of its characters. It is about a state of mind, illusive but real, whose more readily recognizable components are, first, an awareness of America's youth—its undisciplined, swaggering, unregulated early life—and, secondly, a pervasive sense of America in crisis: an America of big-business, of labor strife, of depersonalized government, and, above all, of imminent war. Implicit is the suggestion that, if the nation survives, it will do so by reaffirming certain qualities of its youth and by solving the problems from below, through awareness and good will on the part of the little people. These notions are vague and never articulated, but they are there. In a theater that tends always to overconceptualize, Saroyan's willingness to understate, to rely on implication, and to use character and atmosphere for suggestive power only seemed to many like an evasion of his responsibility. Those who looked for a clearly defined theme and tightly constructed plot were disappointed by the apparent formlessness and the undeniable vagueness of the play. Like *My Heart's in the Highlands,* however, *The Time of Your Life* consists of a mood dramatized, an emotion conveyed directly. It has the power to move an audience, as its response clearly indicated.[6]

The plot is melodramatic—a girl is saved from the clutches of a villainous wretch by a hero whose intentions, by axiom of course, are honorable—but its ironies are multiple: the heroine is a whore; the villain, a law officer; and the hero, inadequate in himself, needs the help of two other men. The innocent one who carries off the girl has no brains; the intelligent one who plans the rescue has no physical prowess; the dauntless one who takes care of the gunplay is an old man of the frontier who still has a pearl-handled revolver and judges shooting according to the self-reliant code of the vigilante. Nevertheless, the play has a hero—who rescues the girl and presumably takes her away to a life of innocence and joy. (She and the innocent one ride away in a truck to San Diego.) That she had become somewhat tainted increased the urgency for returning her to the pristine purity of American womanhood. Paradoxically, in this adaptation of old-time melodrama Saroyan provided a rather sophisticated means for his audiences to indulge their disenchantment with big-city ways and their nostalgia for a simple past.

The Romanticism of this latter-day horse-opera is made palatable to modern tastes not only by its nonchalance and its good-natured spoof of American myths, but also by its motley group of patrons at Nick's who bring variety and timeliness to the play. Presented in a desultory way, these characters help build up a believable, significant *mise en scène.* Though necessarily fragmented as individual portraits, they achieve a notable vitality and at times a sharp satiric edge. A wealthy couple, for example, has left a fashionable supper club to go slumming and has come to Nick's only to observe but cannot remain disengaged. The lady accepts one of Joe's cigars, biting off the tip and lighting up in the manner of Kit Carson, and the man surprises himself by putting in a word for Kitty when she is roughly questioned by the vice-squad officer. Their presence extends the world of the play and helps the theatergoer to take his chair at Nick's, too.

And Willy, who plays the pinball game throughout the entire action of the play, finally asserts his superiority over the machine as one of his marbles strikes home. With frenzied delight, he watches the dance of colored lights; and, as a mechanical arm raises an American flag, he comes to attention and salutes. "Boy, what a beautiful country," he shouts as he collects his six nickels. A more sardonic portrait is that of Dudley R. Bostwick, on whom life is playing a grim joke, for he has been taught that he has a chance in the world. His dignified name stands in amusing contrast to the complete mediocrity of his person. Over the public telephone at Nick's, he professes a great, desperate love for Elsie Mandelspiegel. But his connection is bad, and he pours out his heart to the wrong girl. His essential banality is pointed up further when Elsie finally comes in, for she turns out to be a nurse who has grown bitter through overexposure to sickness, disappointment, and death. In his shallowness and self-interest Dudley simply exploits her pathetic disillusionment. With unglamorous directness she suggests that they go to a cheap hotel together and dream that the world is beautiful.

The pervasive mood of the play is best reflected by Harry, an accomplished dancer who wants to be a comedian although he cannot make people laugh. To McCarthy, a hard-fighting longshoreman with a strike on his hands, Harry's lines are the funniest thing he has ever heard. But he does not laugh and cannot explain why. Actually, no one dares to respond to Harry's humor, for its source is too close to that of tears. It virtually identifies the anguish of the play, having much to do with poverty and the fear of armies:

> I'm up at Sharkey's on Turk Street. It's a quarter to nine, daylight saving. Wednesday, the eleventh. What I've got is a headache and a 1918 nickel. What I want is a cup of coffee. If I buy a cup of coffee with the nickel, I've got to walk home. I've got an eight-ball problem. George the Greek is shooting a game of snooker with Pedro the Filipino. I'm in rags. They're wearing thirty-five dollar suits, made to order. I haven't got a cigarette. They're smoking Bobby Burns panatelas. I'm thinking it over, like I always do. George the Greek is in a tough spot. If I buy a cup of coffee, I'll want another cup. What happens? My ear aches! My ear. George the Greek takes the cue. Chalks it. Studies the table. Touches the cue-ball delicately. Tick. What happens? He makes the three-ball! What do I do? I get confused. I go out and buy a morning paper. What the hell do I want with a morning paper? What I want is a cup of coffee, and a good used car. I go out and buy a morning paper. Thursday, the twelfth. Maybe the headline's about me. I take a quick look. No. The headline is not about me. It's about Hitler. Seven thousand miles away. I'm here. Who the hell is Hitler? Who's behind the eight-ball? I turn around. Everybody's behind the eight-ball!

And this underlying sense of the incongruity of the total human situation which furnishes the basis of Harry's humor is reiterated tersely in the Arab's oft-repeated phrase: "No foundation all the way down the line."

The play has a five-act structure, with the first, third, and fifth acts devoted especially to the plot which I have described above; for the second and fourth acts are designed as supplementary mood pieces. Together they form a kind of "poetic harlequinade"[7] in support of the preface: "in the time of your life, live." But they also produce a reverberating in the mind, suggesting many things. When Blick, the chief of the vice squad, walks in, the atmosphere immediately grows tense. Wesley cannot play, Harry cannot joke. Blick is the villain of melodrama; but in the fall of 1939, when Hitler's armies had begun crushing helpless people, no audience could have missed the implications of authority dehumanized, grown corrupt and sadistic. And we must note that Blick is finally vanquished by a representative of the individualism of America, of a frontier contemptuous of authority and free of vice squads. Kit Carson is an anachronism, but he does what Joe cannot do. It was a brilliant, highly sophisticated touch for the playwright to bring in Kit Carson just before final curtain. "Killed a man once, in San Francisco, name of Glick or Blick or something." In drawling out these words he placed his action in the context of the tall tale, adding credibility to his earlier anecdotes as well as certain fantastic incredibility to what he has just done. Yet he has killed Blick, as the audience knows, and has thrown his pearl-handled revolver into the Bay. Thus the final effect is one of affirmation. The play expresses what its best people feel: it is a wonderful world, after all, as Krupp the Cop puts it, but in our weakness and fear we make a mess of things; sometimes we have to kill to preserve its goodness.

IV Love's Old Sweet Song

Saroyan's next Broadway venture was *Love's Old Sweet Song,* like its predecessor, produced by Eddie Dowling in conjunction with the Theatre Guild. It was directed jointly by Mr. Dowling and the playwright. After a trial performance in Princeton, two weeks in Philadelphia, and one week in Baltimore, it opened in New York at the Plymouth Theatre on May 2, 1940. For its setting Saroyan returned to the San Joaquin Valley, to Bakersfield this time and an old-fashioned house larger and much better maintained than Ben Alexander's in Fresno. The itinerant who happens upon this scene is much closer to the traditional fraud of American folklore than was Jasper MacGregor. Barnaby Gaul is a pitchman, quick-witted and urbane enough to take advantage of the unexpected opportunity of courting under false pretenses Ann Hamilton, the girl who lives alone in this house. Through a spurious message, she has been led to believe that he has secretly loved her for years and has finally returned to Bakersfield to marry her if she will have him. It is an opening scene of astonishing improbabilities, but it sets itself in motion with such breezy confidence that it becomes its own justification. Moreover, it introduces a series of contrasts which Saroyan depends upon for the emotional charge of the play, contrasts which he manipulates adroitly for the central motif as well as for humor.

The first of these contrasts is a message representing an insensitive, treacherous ruse delivered by a boy so tender-hearted that he memorizes collect telegrams and recites them free of charge to their recipients. ("I'm radical," he explains.) And the two leading characters, a spinster and a huckster, are types bearing certain unfavorable connotations which form the bases for surprise when the author later contradicts these expectations. The spinster turns out to be too winsome and defenseless to be the butt of jokes; and, after seemingly confirming the audience's instinctive suspicions of the huckster by revealing his obvious opportunism, Saroyan gives what is surely the big wink when it turns out that this one believes his own pitches: it is not the ingredients of the medicine, he insists, but the faith in its use that counts. But Saroyan's mood is too playful to do no more than turn an apparent bad guy into a good guy; he continues to play an audacious but amusing guessing game with the audience through the ambiguity of his huckster. After all, it is faith that Barnaby is peddling; and, with the help of a message as bogus as his medicine, he first sells Ann Hamilton on it and then to his own surprise decides to buy it himself.

But Saroyan no sooner brings in his two principals than he allows them to be upstaged by a family of "Okies" who descend upon the Hamilton home like a dust storm out of the Southwest. Cabot and Leona Yearling and their fourteen children camp uninvited on the front lawn and finally move into the house itself. "Don't aim to do no harm," says Cabot, "just aim to rest a spell. Leonie's going to have a baby soon, you know." His boys raid the pantry; his girls help themselves to cosmetics and clothes; when his wife appears freshly bathed and dressed in one of Ann's frocks, he makes amorous advances to her, for which he is hit over the head by his half-witted stepson. To this kind of high jinks is added a sheriff of variety-show stupidity who comes on-stage to pronounce the unconscious Cabot dead of accidental causes.

Saroyan's love of caricature was never more ebullient or mischievous. The Yearlings are accompanied by a lady photographer who is gathering material for a picture-story and by a young writer who plans to do a sociological novel. Though the Yearlings firmly refuse all offers of work, Cabot insists that they are migratory workers who have been driven out of Oklahoma by dust; and then he adds nonchalantly, by way of confirmation, "the writer told me." A young man selling subscriptions to *Time* and *Life* chants the names of the editors and their assistants like a rhythmical litany to the saints; Leona begs for an encore and Cabot puts his "X" on the order form. And most astonishing of all such miscellaneous items, the play invokes the better-body craze in the climactic scene when a strongman picks up the pitchman and spins him around in a dazzling display of wrestling holds.

I confess it is hard for me to envision the urbane Walter Huston, who played Barnaby Gaul, flipped and spun about by a Greek wrestler.[8] Whether we consider the incident hilarious or absurd hardly depends on dramatic theory. Suffice it to say that Saroyan managed to relate this breath-taking novelty act to his badly neglected plot—it is punishment administered to Barnaby for having abandoned Ann when the Yearlings moved in. At the same time, Saroyan wisely spared his audience any awkward conjectures about its remedial powers, for Barnaby has come back of his own accord to marry Ann.[9] He has only enough difficulty convincing the Greek of his new intentions to allow for a good measure of gymnastics.

The final scene turns into a travesty of all happy-endings, and as such it is good fun. Barnaby takes his mauling good naturedly; Ann is happy, though she has lost her home, because she has found a lover—and a daughter, too, for she and Barnaby will adopt the youngest Yearling girl, the very child who started the fire that destroyed her house. All the characters come on-stage—except the teen-age Yearling twins who have gone up to San Francisco for a career in harlotry. It would have been well if the stage directions had called for a song and dance at this point, for such a finale might have concealed the play's awkward insistence that its theme be taken seriously. The play is such a genial spoof of everything it touches that it inevitably spoofs its own theme. But Saroyan did not intend to satirize American fondness for happy endings; instead, he asked the audience to accept the power of love to transform the huckster and bring happiness to the spinster, a thesis we would gladly accept tongue-in-cheek in accordance with the spirit of the play, if the author had developed it through the action. As it is, the necessary change is not dramatized. The conflict is introduced in the opening scene, ignored in favor of lively moving vaudeville, and then conveniently swept away in the closing scene. *Love's Old Sweet Song* might have been a success as madcap comedy with satirical dimensions, but as drama it was simply smothered under by vaudeville. The play closed on June 8th, after forty-four New York performances.[10]

On the third of May, however, the night after its opening, the New York drama critics meeting at the Algonquin Hotel voted eleven to seven in favor of *The Time of Your Life* as the best play by an American to open on Broadway during the 1939-1940 season.[11] By consensus they regarded Saroyan as the freshest, most imaginative talent of the time on Broadway. Three days later the Trustees of Columbia University announced that Saroyan had been named for the Pulitzer Prize. (Because he did not believe "in official patronage of art," Saroyan rejected the prize and the thousand dollars which it provided.[12]) Clearly, he was receiving the critical support he had never known before, not even with "The Daring Young Man on the Flying Trapeze." Moreover, the critics were remarkably generous to *Love's Old Sweet Song*. Indeed, going back to these reviews now we might be tempted to think that Saroyan had succeeded in creating a taste for his own kind of sentiment and for his unique mixture of realism and fantasy. More accurately, however, his new play was basking in the favorable critical atmosphere generated by its predecessor; and, even more important, its gentle treatment was made possible by Broadway's hunger for individuality, not to say novelty. Critics were willing to grant this playwright almost any whimsy, however extreme or erratic, as long as he promised to break through the overly conventionalized, imitative patterns of the time. Men like Joseph Wood Krutch, Stark Young, John Mason Brown, George Jean Nathan, and Brooks Atkinson supported him in every way they could. Wolcott Gibbs commented in the *New Yorker*: "Whatever doubts you may have about Mr. Saroyan's status as a formal dramatist, you can't, I think, deny him one of the richest and most fantastic imaginations in the theatre."

At the same time there was general recognition among the critics that *Love's Old Sweet Song* did not effectively employ Saroyan's immense talents. One of them commented charitably that the play was good enough to make him wish it were better. There was a feeling that, however beguiling and gay, the plot left one vaguely dissatisfied. As for audiences in general Saroyan was too far removed from prevailing conventions of the theater. They laughed at the high jinks, but ignored or scorned the message—or so thought Saroyan. This failure in rapport disappointed him deeply. His reaction to what he regarded as their insensitivity tells us how seriously he took this message. It occasioned one of his rare outbursts of bitterness: "In fancy clothes they came by fancy carriage to the opening of *Love's Old Sweet Song*—and soon hissed its truths which were too much for their small minds—and the next minute they applauded. I heard them when they hissed, and I heard them when they applauded, and I have only contempt for them. . . . I wrote it and I directed it and by the time it got to New York it was ready for human beings. It was no affair of mine if they didn't turn out to be human beings."[13]

V The Beautiful People

Love's Old Sweet Song proved to be the turning point in Saroyan's brief career on Broadway. Not that he was ready to give up; but he was determined to dispense with as much professional help as possible. For his next play, *The Beautiful People*, he took over the casting and directing himself and financed the play with money coming in from a successful road tour of *The Time of Your Life* and from wide sales of *My Name is Aram* in the stores and through the Book-of-the-Month Club. Moreover, he discarded what few conventional devices he had used in *Love's Old Sweet Song*, and he returned to the manner of *My*

Heart's in the Highlands. Again he built a play around an incredibly irresponsible family, allowing his fancy to play about the surface of its situation rather than attempting to extend it into a plot.

In *The Beautiful People,* the Websters live in an old house on Red Rock Hill in San Francisco. They get along better than the Alexanders because a pension check comes to them monthly, though its intended recipient, a stranger to them, is dead. The father, Jonah, considers himself a lay preacher and tells Father Hogan, the Catholic priest next door, that he instructs people in much the same way as do the priests from the pulpit. It is Jonah who states what I regard as the theme of the play: "Every life in the world is a miracle, and it's a miracle every minute each of us stays alive, and unless we know this, the experience of living is cheated of the greater part of its wonder and beauty."[14]

In Jonah, Saroyan again found a type richly endowed by the American imagination, only this time he failed to develop its potentials. Instead, he turned to the children of his lay preacher. His seventeen-year-old daughter is called St. Agnes of the Mice by her imaginative younger brother, Owen, who believes that the mice worship her and that at times they spell out her name with little flowers on the parlor floor. He tells how one of them rode downtown on the cow-catcher of a number seventeen street car to get an almond for her. Owen undertakes what is surely one of the most ludicrous quests on record when Agnes announces that one of her mice has disappeared. On the trail of the mouse he goes next door to St. Anne's Church where he falls into the pipe organ. When he finally returns with a live mouse, however, he is told that he has brought back not one of her group but a regular church mouse. Nothing disturbs the family's serenity, however, and after this incident Father Hogan comes in to assure everyone that Owen's fall has not damaged the organ but has actually improved its tone.

Thus the play offers a kind of domesticated tall tale, sometimes amusing in itself but often degenerating into a facetiousness that compromises its theme. Yet Owen is one of the most imaginative and sensitive of Saroyan's characters. Filled with a sense of the glorious mystery of being, Owen writes novels of one word each. His first is the noun "Tree," and he anticipates one day doing a sequel, a two-word novel complete with verb. It is he who gives us the play's most genuine illustration of that miraculous life of which his father speaks, and in so doing he makes possible what little the play offers by way of plot. At the opening, he picks out a tune, "Wonderful One," on the piano, while off-stage the same song is played on a cornet. It is the music of Owen's brother who is three thousand miles away in New York. At the end of the play, the brother returns. There is nothing so prosaic as a causal connection between this return and anything that happens in the play. The reunion is hazardous to describe and folly to lay out on the critic's measuring table; yet it is undeniably effective. Like the best of Saroyan's whimsies, it demands acceptance on its own terms. It inspires Owen to write his first novel of two words. Ecstatically picking up pencil and paper, he writes: "My Brother."

All the characters in the play are Saroyan innocents; there is no villain. The one cloud on the horizon passes harmlessly when the representative of the company that has been supplying the family with checks for the past seven years decides after a visit to the home that everything is in order; indeed, he will recommend an increase in the allowance. This pleasant way of joshing modern finance fits well into the spirit of the play, but it also makes clear why Saroyan had so soon exhausted the dramatic possibilities of his view of man. Unwilling to place his people in the presence of evil, he had no real conflict. Their essential goodness could not be demonstrated; it had to be taken on faith. Though *My Heart's in the Highlands* had no antagonist in the usual sense of the word, it created tensions of its own, as did *The Time of Your Life. Love's Old Sweet Song* posed a conflict in its opening scene which it lost sight of amid the pleasantries of a variety show. Saroyan's fourth Broadway production *The Beautiful People,* though wonderfully fanciful, was totally lacking in tension. We may call it a song, or a lyric poem, but as drama it had no life.

The play remained at the Lyceum Theatre from April 21st until August 2nd, 1941, a run of one hundred and twenty performances which took it out of the red and encouraged Saroyan to consider further productions.[15] Moreover, the play had its supporters among critics, too. At the meeting of the Critic's

Circle in the spring of 1941, the play received six votes as the best play of the year but lost out to Lillian Hellman's *Watch on the Rhine.* Stark Young thought Saroyan's play more pertinent, despite the latter's obvious timeliness: "As to what the final virtue of 'Beautiful People' is, we know, as St. Augustine said of God, if you don't ask us. The everlasting Franciscan is there: love, freedom and finding your own song, intensity and simplicity—the true ghost of our life walking forever under the trees."[16] And Joseph Wood Krutch continued to call attention to the uniqueness of Saroyan:

> Few men ever displayed a completer or more clearly defined set of the stigmata of romanticism. He accepts the universe, believes in the goodness of the human heart, and holds that God is love. He distrusts the respectable, rejoices in the variety of the world, believes in the unique individual, and assumes as self-evident that Beauty is Truth. Above all, he is convinced that the secret of success in both life and art is to let oneself go—as completely and as unthinkably as possible.

Mr. Krutch cautioned against allowing such an analysis to stand as a basis of dismissal; to do so, he added, would be "to remain blind to the primary fact that [his plays] have a freshness of fancy, a gaiety of humor, and a sincerity of sentiment which make them, in my opinion, unique." And he conjectured penetratingly that perhaps Saroyan's "genuine naïveté" derived from an unconcern with the patterns of his convictions that made it possible for him to cherish each one as a fresh revelation to be given "in delightful astonishment" to the world.[17]

But Saroyan could no longer be looked upon as a promising amateur. In general, the critics grew less tolerant of his Romantic optimism the more he continued to ignore customary theatrical form. Reaction to *The Beautiful People* was predominantly unfavorable. In a *New Yorker* review entitled "Well, I Give Up," Wolcott Gibbs dramatized his exasperation by noting that at one point on opening night he had turned to Mrs. Gibbs and had quietly sworn.[18] It was commonly assumed that Saroyan forever improvised, throwing things together thoughtlessly and in haste.

Yet there is nothing hurried about *The Beautiful People.* Indeed, passage after passage shows meticulous attention. This is true of the text, and it was true also of the performance. "I have from watching the scenes," wrote Stark Young in *The New Republic*, "the impression of endless pains, patient indulgence and love spent on rehearsing them." Insisting that this play showed neither "amateur fumbling" nor "non-professional innocence," Mr. Young suggested that one read certain scenes, especially the one in which Owen and a visiting lady talk with one another "like flowers touching their heads together, casual, gentle and wild," and then return to the performance to see how carefully the actors had been coached into this effect of simple personal life.[19] Perhaps it was an act of defiance resulting from disappointment over *Love's Old Sweet Song*, but Saroyan worked hard on *The Beautiful People*, giving it what is probably the most careful, dedicated effort of his dramatic career.

VI *Three One-Act Plays*

The following year, 1942, Saroyan tried his hand at producing and directing two of his own one-act plays. In March, *Across the Board on Tomorrow Morning* had appeared under another's direction at the Theatre Showcase on West 47th Street with Nicolas Evrienov's *Theatre of the Soul* as curtain raiser. Though the response was unfavorable, many felt that Saroyan's play had possibilities that were lost in the performance.[20] Thus the playwright himself took over the play and secured for the leading role the services of Canada Lee, who was fresh from a triumphant performance in the dramatized version of Richard Wright's *Native Son*, and in August the play opened at the Belasco Theatre with *Talking To You* as the companion piece. But Saroyan failed to win critical approval. His production was said to lack proper stylization and punch. Brooks Atkinson, who in March had expressed hopeful interest in the first of these one-acts, conceded that Saroyan failed to bring the play to life in the theater and that *Talking To You* left one with "a generalized, stammering impression." Saroyan needs a professional director, he said flatly, and in this statement he echoed the judgment of many.[21] The play closed after eight performances.

Canada Lee was praised for the quality of sincerity he brought to the part and was in general treated gently by the critics.

Indeed, by this time Saroyan's methods of casting had become something of a legend along Broadway. Rarely respectful of custom, he avoided actors' agents and other usual channels; instead, he searched the streets, the shops, the bars and restaurants, even alcoholic wards to find the right people for his plays; and he showed little concern if these people had never seen the inside of a theater. George Jean Nathan, who shared the prevailing distaste for Saroyan's work as a director, praised with enthusiasm his initiative and vision in casting:

> He sees a strange young girl in a cafe who is the type he needs; he listens to her voice and observes her manner; he hires her on the spot without further ado; and under his confidence a Betsy Blair turns in a beautifully sensitive performance in "The Beautiful People." He sees a colored boy in Harlem who similarly has never been on stage, and a young Armenian cousin of his who has been picking grapes in California, and a hat-check girl at the Stork Club, and a broke poet down in Greenwich Village, and a couple of Filipinos in the Automat, and his "The Time of Your Life" stage is vitalized by a Reginald Beane and a Ross Bagdasarian and his "Across the Board on Tomorrow Morning" is enlivened by a June Hayford, a Maxwell Bodenheim, a Gilbert Advincula and a Sam Sotelo. Nor is it merely type casting. It turns out to be talent casting too. Or at least the odd kind of talent for the peculiar roles that he concocts. And as a consequence a Saroyan stage, however bulky its other deficiences may be, has a newness, a freshness and a simple delight that you won't get from many another stage paraded by talents maybe threefold heftier.[22]

Across the Board on Tomorrow Morning and *Talking to You* had to wait nearly twenty years for the right production. Under the perceptive direction of Arthur Storch, *Two by Saroyan* opened in October, 1961, at the East End Theatre. The intimacy of the small Off-Broadway playhouse contributed measurably to the success of both plays. Equally important to *Across the Board on Tomorrow Morning* was the work of Milt Kamen, who was cast as Thomas Piper, a talkative waiter at Callaghan's bar and restaurant on East 52nd Street, New York. Because Piper also functions as a kind of master of ceremonies, Mr. Kamen's wide experience as supper-club comedian proved to be precisely the right kind of preparation: he was able to maintain an air of easy familiarity with the audience and at the same time catch the spirit of warm-hearted drollery that makes this waiter one of Saroyan's most engaging characters.[23]

One of the extraordinary things about this play is that it eliminates the imaginary fourth wall. Each character on stage discovers the presence of the audience and reacts in his own way—acidly, as does a dignified executive of sixty who comes in with a young girl, assuring her that no one will see them at Callaghan's; or disdainfully, as does an impetuous young man who is wrapped up in anger. Callaghan himself is startled out of his professional urbanity and has to be coached pointedly by Piper before he can play host to his unexpected guests. Using lavish gestures, Callaghan sings "A Harp that Once Through Tara's Halls." Thus Saroyan again combines drama and vaudeville, this time with remarkable effectiveness. It is Piper who first discovers the audience. Trying instinctively to put the guests at ease, he chats amiably about the restaurant, its management and clientele, and about himself, telling how he lost two dollars on a horse named "Tomorrow Morning" and how he has acquired a learned and flexible vocabulary by reading the daily papers, *Time,* the *New Yorker,* and Santayana. Piper is a delightful combination of "intellectual schmalz" and "all-American bonhommie."[24]

Despite similarities to *The Time of Your Life,* the tone of *Across the Board on Tomorrow Morning* is entirely different, and the play never appears repetitious. Throughout the first part, it is brisk and surprising in the best Saroyan manner; it builds up a pleasant and believable café environment, and it conveys wry amusement at man's pretensions. Near the end, however, the play shifts into surrealism: at midnight all existence beyond the doors of Callaghan's comes to an end; nothing exists outside, not even the street. Although the outside world is restored before the final curtain, the tricks involved destroy the true magic of the play. Contrary to what has often been assumed, however, Saroyan was not trying to be philosophical. He was going about the poet's business of proclaiming the miracle of birth and personal identity; again he was urging that in the time of man's life, he should live: bet across the board on "Tomorrow Morning."

Whereas this excursion into surrealism was particularly objectionable when the play first appeared, it is no longer troublesome or especially remarkable to audiences accustomed to the theater of Genet, Ionesco, and Beckett. Taste has in this sense matured to appreciate the play. Likewise, the companion piece *Talking To You* has gained in timeliness because of the recent intensification of concern for racial equality. The dilemma of Saroyan's Negro prizefighter, Blackstone Boulevard, has tragic aspects that were unacknowledged twenty years ago.

The two plays are linked together by the theme of illusion. In *Talking To You,* a blind man says: "I see everything as swiftly as people with eyes, but I don't trust *that* vision, so I wait, I keep blind, inside, as I am outside. I wait until I know I am seeing true."[25] An odd assortment of characters huddle together in a basement room in San Francisco: in addition to the blind man and the Negro, a fighter who cannot win because he refuses to hurt people, there are a deaf boy and a Mexican youth who strums a guitar and sings songs of his own composition. Into their shelter comes an escaped convict, a murderer. Like Blick in *The Time of Your Life,* he radiates evil. The policeman who pursues him is a midget, frozen-faced and terrifying. In the confusion of the chase it is Blackstone Boulevard who is shot, and the little boy is left alone to wonder what is wrong with everybody. The play has some of the characteristics of old-time melodrama, and it lingers too long on the final death scene. But its confrontation of good and evil is sincere and moving, and its title makes clear that every man is involved. At the East End Theatre in the winter of 1961-1962 it was "a frightening allegory of love and hate"[26] played in a setting that had especially disturbing associations for people who had begun to learn about fall-out shelters.

Though this reappearance of conflict in Saroyan's dramatic writing was to be short-lived, it nevertheless provided life-blood for his finest one-act play, *Hello Out There,* which appeared at the Belasco Theatre in September, 1942, a little more than a month after *Talking To You.* Equally severe and uncompromising in its confrontation of good and evil, *Hello Out There* was written with more unswerving singleness of purpose than Saroyan gave to any other play. It has no humor and none of those vagaries of fancy which one expects in his work. The setting is realistic, and the theme is unrelievedly grim. In a small-town jail somewhere on the Southwestern prairie a lone prisoner sits in his cell forlornly tapping on the floor with a spoon, as if he were trying to telegraph words. He is an itinerant gambler who has been charged with raping the wife of a prominent local citizen. Suffering from a head wound inflicted by the enraged husband, he is half-sick, frightened, and intensely lonely. From time to time he cups his hand to his mouth and calls out, "hello out there!"

Eventually he is answered by a young girl who comes in to cook whenever the jail has an inmate. She already knows many things about him, for in an earlier visit she has listened to his semi-conscious mutterings. Their talk grows into a love scene which is poignant, but oddly impersonal; it reveals loneliness and fear rather than passion, and its language, though concrete and colloquial, conveys a generalized emotion:

> All I need is somebody good like you with me. [He says to the girl.] It's no good always walking around in the streets for anything that might be there at the time. You got to have somebody staying with you all the time—through winters when it's cold, and springtime when it's pretty, and summertime when it's nice and hot and you can go swimming—through *all* the times—rain and snow and all the different kinds of weather a man's got to go through before he dies. You got to have somebody who's right. Somebody who knows you, from away back. You got to have somebody who even knows you're wrong but likes you just the same.[27]

The theme of personal isolation so penetrates the entire play that any portion of it—the title, the setting, lines such as those above, and the action—implies the meaning of the whole. Like the prisoner, the girl is "as lonely as a coyote" and feels hopelessly trapped by her surroundings. And the husband, desperately hoping to save face, enters the jail and shoots the prisoner who he knows is innocent, for he must accept his wife's charge of rape or admit her infidelity.

The play was well received. Even Wolcott Gibbs, admitting that he had spoken disrespectfully of Saroyan in former times, called the play "compact, rational, and extremely touching," and spoke of the "curious air of innocent eloquence that pervades the play." Moreover, there was much praise for the performance. Always responsive to Saroyan's best qualities, Eddie Dowling and Julie Haydon teamed up, as they had done in *The Time of Your Life,* to give a highly sensitive reading of the lines. Brooks Atkinson reported that it was "a lyrical performance of great enchantment. His warmth and fervor and her quaint sincerity nourish the lines Saroyan has written and fill his fable with both tender and rebellious emotions."[28]

Hello Out There is uncharacteristic of its author, not because it manifests a tightness of construction or absence of humor, as unusual as these qualities are, but because it reveals a Saroyan in the depth of dismay. Here is an unblinking recognition of man's treachery to man and a disturbing intimation of the mysterious way in which an individual may prove to be his own worst enemy. Saroyan's next Broadway play, *Get Away Old Man,* was also dominated by this dark mood; but this time the author's great power of sympathy was smothered by anger. It is the only play that Saroyan wrote out of personal pique—a reaction to his recent experiences with movie-making in Hollywood—and the result was disastrous. It has professional slickness, but in place of humor there is wit—barbed, brittle, and often forced. Its dialogue is stiff and mannered, and its characters have no life of their own. Even the opening scene lacks the charm and vitality that we have come to expect from a playwright consistently successful with opening scenes. *Get Away Old Man* opened at the Cort Theatre in November, 1943, under the direction of George Abbott, and closed after thirteen performances.

Saroyan's stature as playwright depends upon the work of three years, 1939-1941. As always, he was incredibly prolific; but only those plays that have been professionally produced in New York will be discussed. This choice is justified not only because of what it implies about the excluded plays, but also because of its acknowledgment of Saroyan's own concept, as implied earlier in this chapter, of the play as performance. He has continued to write plays since 1941, of course. In addition to *Get Away Old Man* (1943), there are such plays as *Don't Go Away Mad, Sam Ego's House, A Decent Birth, A Happy Funeral,* all published in 1949, and *The Slaughter of the Innocents* (1952), that have touches of genuine value.[29] They show his usual characteristics of marked individuality, a penchant for provocative titles, and a surprising ability to retain a freshness of mind. But they tend to repeat the weak points of his produced plays without adding any new dimensions.

In retrospect, *Talking to You* and *Hello Out There* take on particular significance, for they show that Saroyan could write out of a keen awareness of evil. The mood which they reflect did not vanish without conscious effort on his part. In 1955 he repudiated *Hello Out There,* calling it "worthless, if not in fact a mistake." Writing in *The Nation,* he said: "As a dramatist, I simply do not believe I have the right to identify human beings as the enemy of human beings. Is there any enemy at all? Is time an enemy? Nature? Change? Loss? Failure? Pain? Death? Not in my thinking. All things, including pain and death, are friends, if for no other reason than that they exist, and the friendship of them must be discovered, measured, understood, and cherished."[30]

Behind these remarks, too remote perhaps for Saroyan to have been immediately aware of its presence, is an Armenian Christianity that asserts itself through the acceptance of suffering, not just as an inevitability to be stoically tolerated, but as a source of spiritual growth which finds its archetype ultimately in the Way of the Cross. It is an attitude that suffuses the entire body of Saroyan's work and accounts in large measure for its distinctiveness. Instinctively he invests human misery with a sense of beauty. Suffering is inevitable and it is beneficial. In *Hello Out There,* only in obvious defeat does the essential resilience of the prisoner's spirit manifest itself. We recall, too, that Johnny Alexander is told that Jasper MacGregor's pain of loss would cease only with his death. Because the people of San Benito Avenue share this pain in varying degrees, a true spirit of community is instantly and beautifully created. They bring food to the old man who in turn pays tribute with his bugle to the longing in their hearts. Homer Macauley and Evan Nazarenus gain maturity and dignity through suffering. When Saroyan writes with absolute sincerity, following the implications of his perception of man's inadequacy in the presence of his sublime possibilities, he is capable of creating a poetry of misery. In his stage directions to *Jim Dandy: Fat Man in a Famine,* he observes: "Prolonged suffering has given everybody in the play dignity, humor and simplicity. Everybody in the play is a miracle."[31]

Yet at the same time this idea of the essential "friendliness of failure" is his greatest weakness as a playwright. The one way in which he might have turned it to valuable account dramatically seemed not to interest him. Had he followed its implications, he might have developed a notion of the "tragical sublime" in which pain and suffering are turned into spiritual triumph, similar in some way perhaps to Schiller's *Mary Stuart* or to the life of Thomas More as recently presented in Robert Bolt's *A Man for All Seasons.* Instead, however, Saroyan turned away from conflict.

VII The Cave Dwellers

His one new play to appear on Broadway since the war, *The Cave Dwellers,* demonstrates effectively both the strength and weakness of his dramatic writing. It is the poetry of suffering that gives dignity and charm to the destitute people, an actress, a clown, and a prize fighter, all "has-beens" who seek shelter in an abandoned theater that is about to be demolished. A number of surprising people wander in during the course of the play: a frightened young girl, a trainer with his performing bear, a pregnant woman who gives birth to her child between the acts, a mute milkman, and a good-hearted boss of the wrecking crew. Their conversation is about the things Saroyan's people usually talk about, such as love, hope, and fear. It is a situation more appropriate to the depression era than to the 1950's, however, and one realizes that what is good about *The Cave Dwellers* has really been given to us before. Although his ever-lively fancy has provided new variations, Saroyan is repeating himself in theme, in manner, and in execution. Moreover, a note of imitation has crept in: there are unmistakable echoes of *Godot.*

But *The Cave Dwellers* is still Saroyan, essentially independent, original in fancy, and inimitable in sentiment. Often it shows the freshness and spontaneity of his first plays. As always, Saroyan believes in his people and is able to make us share his belief. Not the least of the play's merits is that it challenges actors to reach out for those elusive meanings that are so rewarding to cast and audience alike: Barry Jones, the ex-clown wagering his only shoe that he can make a group of rough laborers laugh; Leonie Leontovich reliving her memorable roles; Wayne Morris expressing the awkwardness of a tender-hearted ruffian; and, above all, the exquisitely conceived pantomime part for John Alderman as the mute milkman. It is not surprising that Carmen Capalbo, having achieved a stunning success with *The Three-Penny Opera* at the Theatre de Lys and having undertaken his provocative series at the Bijou Theatre which included *A Moon for the Misbegotten* and *The Potting Shed,* should have been drawn to Saroyan's script. In *The Cave Dwellers,* Carmen Capalbo brought about a fruitful collaboration of actors and playwright. It is a play that had its life in the theater, and in this sense fulfilled what Saroyan envisioned back in 1935 with "Subway Circus."

But the central weakness of *The Cave Dwellers* in the final analysis is the central weakness of *The Beautiful People*: there is no real conflict. To be sure, the play draws tension from the background sounds of wrecking crews and from the heroic resistance of its characters to the dehumanizing force of hunger and cold; but, when the boss of the wrecking crew comes in, he magnanimously grants them a few days grace by sending his men off on sick leave. At one point in the play, the King says: "I cannot be angry . . . This is the world . . . What is the world for? It's for putting up with . . . with humor, if possible. Without excuses, without astonishment, without regret, without shame, without any system and order more elaborate than courtesy and love."[32] However admirable this resignation, it must stand as a substitute in *The Cave Dwellers* for a dramatic resolution.

CHAPTER 5

No Laughing Matter

WHEN SAROYAN turned to drama in 1939, he postponed a question concerning his fiction that had begun to suggest itself with increasing insistence: would the style which he had developed in his short stories prove suitable for the novel? By this time he had reached a high point in his stories—although *My Name is Aram* was published in 1940, much of it had appeared in 1937 and 1938. He had begun to assemble his stories with an eye to unity of theme and, with *Aram,* of setting and character. No longer random collections, his books were beginning to resemble the story-cycle, a form whose vogue had been established by such writers as Sherwood Anderson, in *Winesburg, Ohio* (1919); John Steinbeck, in *Pastures of Heaven* (1932) and *Tortilla Flat* (1935); William Faulkner, in *The Unvanquished* (1938), and *Go Down, Moses,* soon to appear; and Erskine Caldwell, in *Georgia Boy,* which would appear in 1943. Though sufficient unto itself as an art form, the story-cycle seemed less complete than the novel. Saroyan could not long have resisted the more demanding form; for, despite an unmistakable disinclination for sustained discipline, he was a man of creative ebullience with an astonishing capacity for hard work.

I The Human Comedy

His return to fiction after three stormy years on Broadway was caused partly by his quarrel with producers and critics and partly by the outbreak of war. But the precise nature of his departure from the field of drama turned out to be as circumstantial as had been his entrance. Whereas his first play had begun as fiction, his first novel began as drama. In December, 1941, Saroyan moved into an office at Metro-Goldwyn-Mayer in Hollywood with the understanding that he would write "a thoroughly American movie." To the surprise of those who did not know him well, he declined to discuss contracts or salary until his scenario was ready.

In February he finished *The Human Comedy* and the studio, well pleased, paid him sixty-thousand dollars. But at this point difficulties arose, for Saroyan had set his heart on directing the picture and the studio objected. Partly as a warm-up exercise and partly to convince the management of his qualifications, he wrote and produced a short subject, *The Good Job,* based on his own story, "A Number of the Poor." When the studio still remained unreceptive to his wishes to direct *The Human Comedy,* he tried to buy back the script for eighty-thousand dollars; but MGM refused. He gave vent to his anger and disappointment in an explosive article which appeared in *The Daily Variety,* a Hollywood trade paper: "Why I am No Longer at Metro-Goldwyn-Mayer, or the California Shore-Bird in Its Native Habitat, or Brahms Double Concerto in A Minor."[1] *The Human Comedy,* with Mickey Rooney in the lead, became one of the most popular war-time films.

After the movie had gone into production, Saroyan adapted the scenario into a book which his publisher featured as his first novel. *The Human Comedy* enjoyed a greater immediate popularity than did any other of his books. Going back to the novel now, we must remind ourselves that the idea for it began the very month of the Japanese bombing of Pearl Harbor and that it grew into a book during the early period of the war. Published in May, 1943, it was Saroyan's contribution to the national effort at a time when the question of morale was crucial. As such, it offered a good portion of nostalgia for the simple life in what was popularly considered a typical small town, U.S.A., not realistically presented, of course, but softened and purified to represent a way of life to be cherished and defended. Through its central image, the messenger boy, were focused the most representative emotions of the day: the loneliness of separation and the fear of the ever-dreaded message, "The Secretary of War regrets to inform you..."

At the same time, the book encouraged a stiff-upper-lip, not by the usual methods of romanticizing war, or by promising an early end or a better world to follow, but, paradoxically, by inferring that mankind has never been free of war. The point of the book is contained in its Ithaca-in-California motif. Characters are named Homer, Ulysses, Marcus, and the home-town is Ithaca, California—Classical names that call to mind a cultural tradition in which all Americans, even those at its farthest Western shore, are indubitably involved. In his history class, Homer reads about the ancient peoples along the Eastern Mediterranean and learns of the Hebraic-Christian context of his world as well as its Greco-Roman moorings. To this historical dimension is added the reflections of his mother, who assures him that no one nation can be blamed for war, that its cause lies deep in the heart of man; one must not hate the enemy, he is told, but that quality in the enemy which he is trying to control in himself. Thus *The Human Comedy* not only addressed itself to a war-time need for the sense of oneness, but it also offered itself as a guide for a much-needed stoicism by pointing to history and to a philosophy of man. In withholding from its readers the twin pleasures of hating the enemy and of pitying themselves, it rose above the more obvious aspects of war-time propaganda. Its enormous popularity during the war can surprise no one who keeps in mind the emotional needs of the time.

For us today, however, its most valuable part is that which reflects Saroyan's remembered past in Fresno. The book is dedicated to Takoohi Saroyan, the author's mother; and, though the fictional family is Macauley and the town Ithaca, the place and the people are those whom we have met before in his writings. Mrs. Macauley is a widow of two years, her oldest son Marcus has gone to war, her daughter is a restless teen-ager, Homer at fourteen is the fastest Postal Telegraph messenger in town, and Ulysses is four. It is a mutually responsive family, fun-loving, music-loving—one for the most part believable and heart-warming. There are memorable vignettes of Homer buying day-old pies, two for a quarter, and riding swiftly through the streets of the town, of Ulysses visiting the library, watching a gopher push up fresh moist dirt, or waving to the engineer of a passing train. And there is an excellent sketch in the manner of *My Name is Aram* which portrays an Armenian storekeeper who tries to spare his young son the sadness that is in his own heart.

When *The Human Comedy* goes beyond the Macauley family, the scales are tipped unbelievably in favor of the good-guys. Mr. Spangler, who manages the telegraph office; Grogan, the chief operator; Miss Hicks, the history teacher; Big Chris, who extricates Ulysses from a bear trap in the local hardware store—all are beautiful people. The only scoundrel is the high-school track coach who acts like a petty, malicious child; but his evil is so obvious that he poses no real threat to the good people of the book. Indeed, the entire adult world of the town is presented as if it were seen through the eyes of a child, yet the reader is always aware of the author. His omniscient voice narrates the story and the effect is not that of reminiscence but of retrogression from maturity.

The Human Comedy manages to retain a rather tenuous hold on our imagination as long as the war is kept in the background. With the report that Marcus is killed in action, however, we look in vain for any thoroughgoing jarring of the Macauley family's composure. Their adjustment, however consoling it may have been to readers whose sensibilities were exposed to the casualty lists of the daily papers, strikes us today as an implicit denial of the boy's loss. That he will be replaced in their lives by his wounded soldier-buddy who is without family of his own is an idea embraced by the family with too much ease and assurance to be convincing. Moreover, the message and its consequences, because they constitute the climax and resolution of the novel, undermine its central conflict and thus weaken the effect of everything that has gone before. Without these novelistic devices, then, *The Human Comedy* might have held its own as a rather winsome cycle of stories, unified in time, place, and character, and expertly told in some of its episodes; but the author was not ready to bring the real war into his fiction nor to shape his materials effectively into the form of the novel.

II *Twin Adventures*

But for Saroyan himself the war was not to remain in the background. About five months after leaving Metro-Goldwyn-Mayer, he entered the army and began a period of service that lasted until the fall of 1945 and included thirteen months of overseas duty. While in London with an army film unit, he wrote *The Adventures of Wesley Jackson,* a novel about an American soldier who takes basic training in California, serves with the Signal Corps in the United States and England, takes part in the invasion of France, falls into enemy hands, and is freed by the Allied advance. Although at the time of the writing, summer of 1944, Saroyan himself had experienced most of the noncombatant aspects of this story—the battlefield and prison camp occupy a small portion only—he was unable to get the atmosphere of war into the pages of his book. Indeed, his instinctive aversion for this new story material is indicated by the fact that for the first time in his career he deliberately wrote with his eye on another book; he chose as a guide for his protagonist that classic outsider, Huckleberry Finn.

With this model in view, his second novel inevitably became an experiment in the picaresque. It was a mode which involved him, on the one hand, in the problem of finding within the rigidities of war-time military life the necessary freedom of movement for his *pícaro* and, on the other, in the equally fundamental problem of his own temperamental inability to maintain the authorial distance required by this genre. Wesley conducts himself with unabashed indifference to army regulations, and early in the story he manages to trick the army into treating him to a joyride to Alaska and back. Soon the nineteen-year-old recruit becomes indistinguishable from the thirty-six-year-old author, and the boy loses the straight-faced drollery that is the most valuable potential of the *pícaro*. Moreover, the author's own experiences in the service, as well as his recent reversals on Broadway and in Hollywood, had obviously dimmed his characteristic geniality and optimism. Never one to force a mood, he was unable to catch the right tone for the picaresque: where it should have been flippant, it was tight-lipped and grim; where it should have been sardonic, if not cynical, it was sentimental.

Not that Saroyan was without his usual *bonhomie* when it came to drunks, streetwalkers, down-and-outers of all kinds—even to the war-time enemy—but his good nature no longer extended to all people. Military officials, especially those with commissions, were beyond the range of tolerance. The novel portrays them not satirically but peevishly, as it does the movie-makers with whom Wesley must confer while he is serving with a training film unit of the Signal Corps. The enlisted men up front, on the other hand, are among the beautiful people. Their spirit of fraternity reaches across the front lines. In the scuffle that leads to Wesley's capture, the Germans are careful not to hurt anybody; they shoot only the man in Wesley's group who resists capture. They treat their captives courteously, take only a few of their coveted cigarettes. At the prison compound the guards who have picked up a little English chat amicably "about the same old things–home and girls and our side and your side and to hell with all Armies, take a look at my daughter, have you anything to swap?" One evening a prisoner from Cincinnati entertains the entire camp, guards and prisoners alike, with the music of his trombone. "I don't know what's American as against what's something else," says Wesley, "but I know there is no man in the world capable of resisting truth and beauty like the truth and beauty that came out of Wynstanley's trombone on the evening and night of Saturday, July 22, 1944."[2]

As in *The Human Comedy,* the resolution is much too easy to be convincing; it does not come through pain and suffering but is simply asserted in bland disregard of these realities. Wesley is no descendant of Huck Finn. Deficient as an observer, he is in fact so manifestly indifferent to war, either as personal challenge or as national conflict, that he becomes a protagonist of almost unbelievable shallowness. Throughout the entire book his one ambition has been to find a girl who will bear him a son. That he succeeds in doing so can be of little interest to most readers.

Publication of *The Adventures of Wesley Jackson* was withheld until 1946 when the nation was ready for a peace-loving novel that ended with the happy reunion of the soldier and his bride. That it was issued again in 1950 as part of a volume called *Twin Adventures,* the companion piece consisting of a diary that Saroyan kept during its writing, indicates how strong were the author's compulsion to publish and the publisher's reliance on a continuing demand for his work, no matter how hastily tossed off. The day-by-day chronicle of his adventures at the typewriter points up the least fortunate aspects of his attitude toward writing. With no genuine commitment to the story material at hand, his greatest concern was that he finish the novel within the time limit he had set for himself—one month. The diary records his alternating seizures of exhilaration and discouragement, the latter nearly always a result of fatigue alone; enemy bombs that occasionally fell in his neighborhood are no more distracting to this preoccupied author than are problems of laundry and interruptions of well-meaning friends. The diary makes all too clear that Saroyan was taking himself very seriously as a writer without really respecting what he wrote. With "The Adventures of William Saroyan," as he calls it, he has inadvertently written a mock-heroic that becomes at times unintended self-mockery.

III Dear Baby

In order to account for Saroyan's state of mind during the summer of 1944 one must go not to the diary but to the collection of short stories, *Dear Baby*, the first since *Aram*, which he brought together just before beginning *Wesley Jackson*. Although drawn from earlier material—its title piece had appeared in *Collier's* in 1939 and some of its stories date from 1935—this slender volume does much to explain the author's detachment from the immediate issues of the war. Death and melancholy predominate in these stories, but they are there to underscore the beauty and evanescence of each moment of life. One of its titles, for example, is "The Hummingbird that Lived through the Winter"; and another, "Knife-like, Flower-like, Like Nothing at all in the World." In a sketch called "How It Is To Be," the author tells of a visit with his grandmother in Fresno. There is almost no description of the scene; but, through the suggestive power of a few specific nouns, Saroyan evokes a way of life that implies its own cultural history. The two lunch on Armenian bread and cheese, and on lamb and rice wrapped in vine leaves. The atmosphere is ancient, Eastern, and mystical in the two-fold sense of a yearning for the "wholly other" and a feeling of helplessness before the eternal mysteries of life and death: "Men are miraculously living things, never more than a day from death, only visitors of the world, borrowers of time, not possessors of anything but the privilege of inhabiting substance and enduring time."[3] This attitude has little to do with formal religious thought, or with the "thou-shalt-nots" of moral system. Indeed, it prevails despite an underlying scepticism and a surface gloss of Western sophistication; and it tends to stand apart from temporal issues.

The sketch helps explain, too, why Saroyan attached so much importance to a childlike freshness of response. The old man, he says, leaves the world as helplessly as he entered it. In this sense, living is always in its infancy. There is an aura of mysticism about this view, whether the reader chooses to regard it as a part of Romanticism in the West or as traditionally Christian, in which the altar of God is forever the joy of one's youth. All *true* writing, Saroyan believed, expresses a spontaneity of apprehension.[4]

IV The Assyrian

What the loss in freshness of response would mean to his own writing was to occupy his thoughts during the next few years and inspire more genuine self-analysis than he had ever before known. Whereas most of his numerous attempts to explain himself to his readers had done little more than reflect transient moods, his first post-World War II book, *The Assyrian and Other Stories*, is comparable to *The Daring Young Man on the Flying Trapeze* and *My Name is Aram* in the light it throws on Saroyan's art. The Preface and the two most distinctive stories are filled with the author's concern for the fundamental problem of his own growth.[5] He saw clearly that, like many young writers, he had often gotten by on exuberance alone. Exuberance soon vanished, he realized, and even at best it was not enough—unless, he thought, one was a Thomas Wolfe.[6] On the other hand, he had to admit that, despite his past efforts to master a form somewhere between the personal essay and the short story, he had never been interested in form as such. He had not wished to paint word pictures or to write about things that occupied most writers of fiction. Though he had come to respect professionally competent writing, it often seemed to him "to have been made by a fine piece of machinery instead of by a human being."[7]

For better or for worse, he knew, this "human being" within his own work had been irrepressible: "Either I myself was the beginning and end of the matter, or there was no matter at all." Though this comment fails to recognize the power of his best fiction to transcend the self, his stock-taking was essentially accurate: "I wanted to say something about myself, and something about the effect people I happened to run into, including my family, had on me." This is a casual way of acknowledging the influence of others, but his egocentricity had now become less flamboyant and more reflective. He understood that the real question for himself as author amounted to whether he would continue in the manner of his pre-war days or would reach out for those new things that came to him as he grew older: "A man can always go after the tough stuff—the stuff that's so hard to put into the form of the short-story or novel—in his private life . . . and never go after it in his writing, never take a chance on it."[8]

Some of the stories of *The Assyrian and Other Stories* do not go after the new things. Of "The Parsley Garden," which tells how an eleven-year-old boy wins back his self-respect after being guilty of shoplifting, Saroyan said: it is "another item out of the miscellaneous past."[9] He was "playing safe," as he put it; but the story is specifically imagined, strongly felt, and enriched by an oblique use of the garden symbol. In "The Pheasant Hunter" and in "The Cornet Player," however, the familiar Fresno material has hardened into formula. Mechanical, too, is "The Theological Student," which presents Aram Garoghlanian, now fourteen and interested in Russian novels and Soren Kierkegaard. But the boy lacks the spark of his namesake, and the many uncles squeezed into the story become travesties of those we know from *My Name is Aram.*

Other stories are set in a world no longer as familiar as that of Aram. It is a world where the American of Near-Eastern background is unable to unify his sensibilities according to Western patterns of thought and response. This dichotomy, profoundly unsettling to Saroyan, is nowhere more clearly presented than in his first post-war story, *The Assyrian,* a novella of thirty thousand words. Autobiographical in the general way of "The Daring Young Man," its protagonist is a writer of fifty. As in the earlier story, he is keenly aware of failure, but now he is quite willing to look within himself for the cause. The feeling of aloneness is no longer associated with personal eccentricity or with society's indifference to the artist. Paul Scott, the protagonist, is Assyrian on his mother's side, the side that was steadily emerging in his consciousness:[10]

> The longer he'd lived the more he'd become acquainted with the Assyrian side, the old side, the tired side, the impatient side, the side he had never suspected existed in himself until he was thirteen and had begun to be a man. It was then that he had learned to speak the strange and almost impossible language, staying at the homes of his mother's relatives, listening with them to the phonograph records of the songs of the old country—the songs of all the peoples of that part of the world—singing the songs, speaking the language as if it were a secret shared by only a handful of people miraculously salvaged out of an extinct race. Even his skin began to grow dark when he became a man, and he encouraged his cousins to call him by his Assyrian name, Belus Alahabad, and he began to understand how superior he must be to most other people in that his very race was finished and had no need to clamor for irrelevant rights of any kind.

Paul Scott is himself a visitor of the world in the sense referred to in the autobiographical sketch above, and he knows that his borrowed time is fast running out. Three unsuccessful marriages have left him haunted by his inability to find lasting love. What he remembers most clearly about his past affairs is the reading of *The Rubaiyat of Omar Khayyam* with a girl whom he knew briefly in San Francisco. In Lisbon, he learns that his heart is perilously weak. Like the writer in Henry James's "The Middle Years," Paul has to face the fact that there will be no later phase. To fill the hours, he gambles recklessly in nearby Estoril and flirts with the sophisticated daughter of a Lisbon art critic. But his desperate feeling of aloneness is eased only when he converses with Curti Urumiya, an elderly Assyrian who like himself is international in perspective and connections but exclusively Asia Minor in his heart's core. Surviving a severe heart attack one night in the lobby of the hotel, Paul Scott manages to take a cab to the airport and board a plane for the East. This final symbolic gesture is anticipated by the story's epigraph, a tribute to the East and to human longing for "the regions beyond the Euphrates, to which history and tradition point as the birthplace of the wisdom of the West . . . to the ancient seats of civilization which religion has made holy."

With a renewed awareness of heritage, Saroyan achieved a surer perspective of his past work and a confidence in his search for new direcitons. "I myself am a product of Asia Minor," he said, "hence the allegorical and the real are closely related in my mind."[11] Having grown up in a literary environment dominated by Realism he had never before recognized the allegorical nature of his own idea of art. Now he was in a better position to see why he had instinctively avoided ugliness and violence in his writing and had left himself open to charges of softness. It was not just sentimentality or a matter of temperament; allegory has no obligation to portray life as it is but only to select that which illustrates its themes. Though his Preface does not discuss the nature of allegory, his comments on the stories of *The Assyrian and other Stories* attest implicitly to a new respect for the prerogatives of selection. What he liked about "The Parsley Garden," for example, was that "the words of such writing only *imply* the real story."[12] The literal was there not to represent but to suggest the essential note of the allegorical. Most certainly Paul Scott is much more than an individual who is trying to outrun death. He is a dying member of a dying race; and his instinct to return to the source of his being is filled with implications of a kind which Saroyan had hinted at in *My Heart's in the Highlands,* but had never before attempted with this seriousness of purpose.

Not long before writing *The Assyrian* Saroyan had met Ernest Hemingway in London in 1944 and in Paris in 1945.[13] The Hemingway style had long been an ideal for him, but Saroyan disclaimed any direct influence and, for reasons of temperament, could never approach its toughness and restraint. But there are conscious imitations in his early work, as I have shown, and with painstaking effort he had striven to make the clipped dialogue and sparing use of descriptions and narration distinctive marks of his own style. *The Assyrian* presents the anomaly of an experienced writer reverting to an obviously derivative manner, for he found his pattern in "The Snows of Kilimanjaro," to express attitudes authentically and inimitably his own. The similarities between the two stories are many. Beyond those of the central situation and the symbolic plane ride are the bitter-sweet reveries of the dying men, their irrepressible appetites, and their recognition of the connection between failure as human beings and failure as writers. Yet the over-all effect of *The Assyrian* is authentic, for it expresses Saroyan's important and most serious theme, and does so with a nervous, tense style that communicates the inner turbulence of a vital person who feels his life slipping away.

It was the one story of the collection which he "most needed to write," Saroyan said.[14] This remark has considerable validity, because with *The Assyrian* he opened a vein that was to occupy his best attentions for several years and lead in 1953 to his most dedicated attempt to write a tragic novel. Also noteworthy for its pivotal position is a companion piece, "The Cocktail Party." Andrew Loring, an aging author, is depressed by an apparent impasse in his career. His painful reappraisal of himself and his work reveals his loss in creative exuberance. However, he resolves to make the most of that which is yet his. A resolution suggestive of Omar, it is Westernized in its desire to put life's remaining moments to constructive use. Though less dramatic and much less ambitious than *The Assyrian,* "The Cocktail Party" manages to make its point while seeming to do little at all. Moreover, it has valuable overtones about the importance of love to continued growth. Although Andrew Loring is in some ways more distinct from Saroyan than are his other fictional authors, the story's climax carries an unmistakable ring of personal resolution, suggesting on Saroyan's part a rededication to creative activity and a determination to write out of his contemporary self. Certainly, the pace of his publishing picked up at this point. He had published no book of fiction between *Wesley Jackson* (1946) and *The Assyrian* (1950), a long pause for this writer; but in 1951 he published two novels.

V Rock Wagram

The first of these, *Rock Wagram,* is a novel of self-discovery. Arak Vagramian is a happy-go-lucky bartender in Fresno until one day a visiting film dignitary spots his potentials as a movie personality and takes him off to Hollywood. As Rock Wagram he becomes a star in pictures that are popular but as spurious as his new public personality. After a time, however, he realizes that he can never submerge himself happily in this new image and returns to the place of his birth in a ritualistic, instinctive effort to get in touch once more with his true self. He drives compulsively day and night until he reaches his home. After visiting the familiar scenes, he turns to his young cousin and says: "Well, boy, I'm in Fresno, I've been to the house on Winery Street, I slept there last night, had breakfast there this morning. . . . We've been to the red-brick church, we've lighted candles, we've prayed, we've been to *The Asbarez,* we've talked, and now we're at Fat Aram's."

The jaunty manner of this pronouncement does not disguise the essential solemnity of the young man's mission: he is a pilgrim at a shrine. At the office of *The Asbarez,* the Armenian newspaper where Rock's father had worked many years earlier, he and his cousin talk with Krikorian Ahpet, who for thirty years has been editor, writer, typesetter, and janitor of the twice-weekly paper. The old man paraphrases in English for his two visitors an Armenian poem which had been composed by the elder Vagramian and dedicated to his younger son:

> Here is a world in which I am a stranger, given to me by a stranger, my own father. I give it to you, my own son Haig, and a stranger. . . . Would God this world were better and more, and you and I not strangers, for I love you, I love you so deeply that my love estranges you from me, me from myself, and love itself from love.

The search for the father is central to the book's theme, and its religious implications, though tenuous, are provided for as they are not elsewhere in Saroyan's work. It is through an Armenian priest that Rock comes to understand the meaning of family in terms of continuity of values. In a conversation that becomes the climax of the main plot and makes possible the resolution of the supporting plot, Father Zadik interprets for him his father's poems of love. Like most Armenians in Fresno, what Rock most wants is a vineyard and family, and for these things he would gladly exchange his career as a movie star.[15] But his wife no longer loves him. His love for her is strong, but the gulf between them in years, family background, and temperament is great, and he has ceased to respect what she holds dear. His challenge lies in self-discipline: he must accept his broken marriage, learn to live without his wife and two children and yet continue loving and serving them in any way he can. The resolution is similar in spirit and tone to that of "The Cocktail Party."

The inferences to be drawn from *Rock Wagram* relate broadly to an American problem. To Saroyan the protagonist's failure to organize himself within the diversities of his new life suggested the need of second-generation Americans to open themselves to the varieties of thought and custom without rejecting those values that are fundamental to their particular ethnic group. He has portrayed others in the book who never knew the painful soul-searching of Rock Wagram. Some of Rock's cousins are content to isolate themselves within the well-knit, self-contained group and never enter the mainstream of American life. They offer no solution to America's problem of cultural synthesis. But there is the contrary hazard, too, that is pointed up eloquently by a foil to Rock, Craig J. Adams, who is also descended from the Vagramians, but has buried his past, forgotten all things Armenian, and is interested in Rock only out of reverence for success. He is a type of new American, sophisticated but shallow.

Rock Wagram should be better than it is. Its novelistic devices are handled competently: there are two main strands to the plot, each presents an important aspect of Rock's personal conflict; and the climax of one provides the resolution for the other. Character is defined through action, and the conflict and crisis leave the protagonist significantly changed. The novel is much weaker, however, when it considers the swish drawing rooms and cocktail lounges of Hollywood and New York, scenes which Saroyan never learned to get right. The conversations are often brash and at times incredibly naïve. But a more serious flaw belies Saroyan's lack of faith in the story elements to do their own work. Much of the action unfolds within the consciousness of the central figure, upon whose growing awareness the novel rightly focuses. But Saroyan has allowed the necessary passages of reflection to become impossibly intrusive. The movement of the story is retarded by countless italicized comments that cease to be projected musings of a protagonist and become repetitive and dull authorial preachments.

The novel was not well received. One reviewer objected to what he called "the earnest-sounding mindlessness" of the book: "There is no other novelist in the same echelon of talent as Saroyan who can pack so much silliness between the covers of a book."[16] What the reviewers missed, however, was what Saroyan's Armenian background brought to the novel and proves in retrospect to be its best element. Its vagueness after all is Eastern and mystical, and therefore alien to Western preferences for precision and clarity. Nelson Algren, who had serious reservations about the novel, noted particularly that Saroyan is "a man who says a great deal that washes nothing but his old laundry." But Algren also saw its universal aspect: Rock Wagram's love for his young wife "is the love of all men for all women as his love of a long-dead brother is a love of all dead brothers." It is, he says, quoting from the novel, the romance of all men moving "through a mournful dream seeking many things, but in the end they are all only one thing: the Word, and nothing in the lonely world is lonelier, for the name of the Word is Love."[17]

VI Tracy's Tiger

The same year, 1951, Saroyan published a fantasy, *Tracy's Tiger,* which contrasts pleasantly with *Rock Wagram.* Tom Tracy is an ordinary fellow, a San Franciscan who has come to New York and taken a job hustling coffee sacks in a warehouse. Like most people, Tracy has a tiger. It helps him through crises and at times leads to surprisingly bold actions, as when Tracy storms into the boss's office to demand the job of coffee taster. But the complication of the story sets in when Tracy finds himself kissing his girl's mother, and not in the dutiful manner of a prospective son-in-law. Tracy scolds his tiger sternly, but the damage has been done and he returns despondently to San Francisco.

Eventually he comes back to New York. By this time, however, his tiger has begun to show itself frequently. One day on Fifth Avenue Tracy is surprised when people begin to flee at his approach. Police cars gather, and an armed man shouts orders through a megaphone. There are gun shots, but the tiger escapes. Tracy is taken to Bellevue, which is filled with people who have lost love. He answers all questions courteously. Through the sympathy and good sense of a police captain and a psychiatrist from Vienna, he is permitted as an experiment to return to the coffee warehouse and the neighborhood where he had met and courted his girl. The tiger, wounded and very much subdued, rejoins him; but Tracy is able to get back his girl. Needless to say, in exchange for the privilege of living happily-ever-after, Tracy has to give up his tiger.

Tracy's Tiger has a swift, buoyant style. In centering on a return to the past, the plot conforms neatly to an accepted technique of psychotherapy. It is timely, too, in its tongue-in-cheek concession to mythology; for, as Thomas Sugrue noted, Saroyan was engaging in a little myth-making of his own in giving us "a journey of search within the hero's psyche as if it were a series of happenings in the physical world."[18] Moreover, with this book Saroyan charmingly spoofs his own preoccupation with the themes of lost love and with the recovery of the past, winks good-naturedly at his growing fondness for allegory, and at the same time laughs at pretension and Western devotion to efficiency and control.

VII The Laughing Matter

After this pleasant respite, however, he turned once more to a serious confrontation of the conflict that had occupied him in *The Assyrian* and *Rock Wagram.* In *The Laughing Matter* (1953), he followed out the tragic potentials of estrangement with unrelenting consistency and economy of means. It is the most closely reasoned, deeply felt, and carefully written of his novels.

Evan Nazarenus, an instructor at Stanford University, has just completed a summer session as guest lecturer at the University of Nebraska and is eager to be reunited with his wife, Swan, and their two children, Red and Eva. He brings his family to the nearby San Joaquin Valley for a late summer vacation. On the first evening there, while he and his wife are having drinks together, she tells him that she is pregnant by another man. In fierce and uncontrollable rage he strikes her and goes off wildly to San Francisco to talk with his brother Dade. His marriage had seemed to him a good one. The shock of discovering that he and his wife were strangers to each other, however, awakens him to the pathos of her personal isolation. "She's got no family," he tells Dade. "She's got an aunt in Philadelphia that she lived with until she was seventeen. She's never had parents or a home . . . She's been looking for parents and a home all her life. That was the idea of the vineyard—to get her a home and a family . . . and a husband who could love her the way she is. What good is love if it isn't entire?"

Resolving to maintain an outward composure for the sake of the children and to await the time when he can face decisions calmly, he returns immediately to his family. The youngsters are responsive to the charged atmosphere, however; and, if they talk too maturely and know too much, as some reviewers have claimed, their susceptibility to tension and their vulnerability are painfully plausible. It is devotion to family and to the idea of familial continuity that deepen Evan's disappointment and turn it into a sometimes frenzied fear, that, like his father and his brother, he too would fail to get roots down in America. Evan and his brother often speak the Armenian tongue together, and Evan is eager to teach it to Red. "Teach him the language in thoughts," cautions Dade, "not in words." The brothers remember their father, Petrus, who had come to America to build a new life. Their mother had died shortly after the birth of her second son, and their father had become "a sad old man in a silly little cigar store in Patterson, New Jersey, living for his sons."

What went wrong? Evan insistently asks of his brother. Evan knew that within his heart there was the power to forgive his wife and the will to love her as she is. "She begged me," he later confessed to Dade, "but I wouldn't listen to her." Instead, he phoned Dade and asked him to arrange an abortion. The consequences of this climactic decision come with breath-taking rapidity. Swan dies, not from the operation, as Evan at first believes, but from an excess of sleeping pills. Insane with grief, Evan shoots his brother and is himself killed when his car goes off a mountain road. Trapped in the overturned car, he hears flames which he thinks of as tongues of laughter: not hysterical or terrified laughter, but sardonic, self-humiliating laughter that sums up the book's ironic view of failure.

The use of irony in the title and in the last scene is the book's only means of relieving emotional intensity; and, because irony shares with tragedy a consciousness of disparity between what man reaches for and what he gets, it does this without contradicting the tragic nature of the novel. It has the effect, however, of dissolving any pessimism that inheres in the novel's picture of human weakness. Moreover, it is indeed an appropriate mode for presenting the fall of a man who lacks the stature of the traditional tragic hero and whose flaw is an uninspiring absorption in self, if self be allowed to include that other version of one's identity, the brother.

For Saroyan, personal isolation, not death, is the essential tragedy. It is restlessness of heart, irremediably aggravated in the sensitive person by cultural uprooting, that brought him his most troubled moments. Evan Nazarenus, like Rock Wagram, wanted "to drive night and day" to get back to the house his father had built and walk through the streets of his boyhood. Why this pervasive strain of melancholy remains free of pessimism is never made explicit in Saroyan's writing, but it implies a persistence of Armenian Christianity. One might recall his observation in the preface of *The Daring Young Man* to the effect that we could laugh at many things if we would remember that we are as good as dead. This ironic view, always characteristic, deepened with the years. The death of Paul Scott, the Assyrian, is less important than his instinct to return to the source of his being. Evan Nazarenus says: "We live in error every day and correct not one error in a lifetime." But Evan's experience illustrates a truth which both he and his brother come to see clearly: the greatest error is "to live a life of pride," for that is what separates man from man.[19] Evan had been deficient in love, but he died loving. And to Saroyan this makes all the difference.

The Laughing Matter is surprisingly Classic in form. The plot and subplot are precisely defined yet deftly interrelated in their development. The setting is not described but named and commented on by the characters so that it exists primarily in its impingement upon their emotions. The vineyard becomes a kind of norm against which one sees the willfulness and caprice of man. Thus the setting, though tangible and specific, is also a pervasive symbol, one that is enriched by an unobtrusive suggestion of the archetypal Garden and Fall. In style, Saroyan avoided narration and description, and employed a staccato dialogue as a means of communicating the turbulent emotions that lay just beneath the surface of the Nazarenus family life. Unfortunately, this staccato is so unrelieved that it becomes jarring to the reader, draws undue attention to itself, and makes all characters talk alike.

VIII *The Allegorical Vision*

On the whole, *The Laughing Matter* received fair and responsive treatment from reviewers. They praised the novel for the obvious care with which it was written and for the tautness of its organization. John Brooks wrote: "Strong feeling is leashed by a sense of form. Sharp scenes, some of them almost unbearably moving, and a fast-moving story are the result. The way the neighbor couple and their children are used as a sort of Greek chorus to the main story is valid and compelling." And Elizabeth Bowen noted "the summer lightning of fantasy" that flickers through the scenes. But their final verdict was unfavorable, as it was with most reviewers.[20]

Charges of arbitrariness in plotting that were brought against the book throw more light on the literary fashions of our day than upon any weakness in Saroyan. The reviewers failed to see the allegorical nature of the book, for Saroyan had assumed this nature so automatically that he had failed to provide sufficient clues. Only by placing this book in its context with the *novella The Assyrian, Tracy's Tiger,* and *Rock Wagram* can we appreciate the extent to which the allegorical habit of mind was controlling his artistic conception. One reviewer complained that Saroyan did not root his catastrophes in the motivations of his characters. It is true that the actions of his characters are not motivated in the sense of specific plot arrangement. But if it is arbitrary, it is so in the way of the ancient fable. Saroyan's purpose was to illustrate a general truth, to set forth a condition rather than to develop an action. His motivations are based on limitations inherent in human nature, and the real strength of his book lies in its power to suggest that vice is its own punishment: defective love and the inability to forgive are ugly in themselves, and they defeat marriage. Seen in this light, the catastrophes are inevitable and convincing, and their presence is felt throughout the entire book.

In *Rock Wagram* and in *The Laughing Matter* the protagonist does not find his woman, he *creates* her. The woman is eternally elusive because she is envisioned in terms of what he lacks. Thus the unfulfilled love takes on the aspect of a universal quest and is moving to the reader far beyond the impact of one man's disenchantment. Yet, at the same time, the reader misses the fullness of person which he has come to expect in the novel. *The Laughing Matter* suffers, not through imprecision—as some reviewers have thought—but surprisingly enough through the bareness of its abstractions: Evan is seen only as a series of attitudes and fears, and Swan has no existence of her own.

The sequence which closes with these two books is crucial in the post-war career of Saroyan. It has all the advantages of a theme that is part of the life-blood of the author, one on which he lavished great care and remarkable skill so that each book is a decided improvement over its predecessor. There is a paradox to this sequence, however. Because of its competence and dedication, it demonstrates that Saroyan would probably never achieve an order of success in the novel equal to that of his short fiction and his fantasies for the stage. In style, he lacks the necessary suppleness and range, and in temperament he is without the circumspective habits of mind and interest in character for its own sake that are the novelist's principal stock in trade. Since 1953 Saroyan has attempted no more serious novels.

CHAPTER 6

The Afternoon of the World

I *Saroyan in a Changing World*

IN THE SEQUENCE that began with *The Assyrian and Other Stories* and ended with *The Laughing Matter* Saroyan tested the range and power of his art with an intensity and seriousness of purpose far beyond anything he had done before or has done since. Thus the sequence is not only especially illuminating in itself but it is also decisive in respect to the kind of writing he has done since 1953.

The attitudes toward theme and technique expressed in *The Assyrian* were much the same as those of *The Daring Young Man*. The center of his writing, he knew, would continue to be his own personality and its general contours those of his own life. At the same time, he had developed a surer sense of the general truth implicit in the particular fact and a greater respect for the knack of getting across what is left unsaid. Like his own Andrew Loring in "The Cocktail Party," he had resolved that however the years might assault his sensibilities and diminish his powers he would continue to use what was yet his to spend. Fearing the limiting consequences of nostalgia, he concluded that whatever proved insuppressible in his remembered past he would try to put into the service of his contemporary self. Thus with *Rock Wagram* and *The Laughing Matter*, as with *The Assyrian*, he went after the new awareness; and in the deeply troublesome post-war years this meant a search for the father image that became more elusive as the world of Aram Garoghlanian receded into the past.

In part, the sequence was an experiment to test the suitability of his style for the longer forms of fiction and, more fundamentally, to find a way out of the impasse which he faced in the years immediately following World War II. To understand the gravity of this impasse, we must recall how closely bound up with milieu was Saroyan's initial success. Those qualities of his art that had been largely instrumental in this success were precisely those that made it so difficult to adapt to the changes that took place during and immediately after the war. The expansion and prosperity of post-war America were in their way as unmalleable for Saroyan's imagination as was the war itself.

Although Saroyan was twenty-one when the financial crash of 1929 ended the prosperity of the 1920's, he had never known the jazz-age aspects of this period. For him it had been a time of peddling papers, working in vineyards, delivering telegrams, and in other ways sharing the family struggle against poverty. By the time the Great Depression had reduced a large part of the nation to resentment and fear, Saroyan had acquired a nonchalance toward hardship that was good-natured, well tested, and, in its context, enviable. Moreover, it was steadied and given perspective by an inherited Armenian habit of regarding privation and struggle as inseparable from the human condition. Thus his writing was remarkably free of animosity and the imputations of class struggle. Instead it exhibited the more enduring qualities of acceptance, unique in the writing of a young man and especially so in a time of protest and reform. The ambience was precisely right for this young writer: it aroused his sympathies, quickened his imagination, and, as a much-needed balance for his affirmations, it provided him with an all-pervasive conflict, made immediate and vivid by the immigrants and transients of Fresno and San Francisco.

When the nation turned to war, Saroyan served in the army and drew upon war for his first two novels. But the conflict of man against man, especially when organized by governments, repelled his creative instincts. A deep psychological barrier, deriving perhaps from the tragedy of Armenia which echoed in the family memory, made it impossible for him to force his imagination to embrace what he had assumed would be his new subject. In attempting to bring the war directly into the idyllic lives of the Macauleys, he seriously weakened his first novel. In his second novel he put his protagonist in uniform, sent him to the front and to a prison compound; but nothing could demonstrate more emphatically the automatic recoil of imagination from the reality of war. It was not haste that defeated Saroyan in this novel; nor was it the form itself, for he handled competently such novelistic devices as the flashback, the exchange of letters, and the swiftness of pace necessary to the episodic structure of the picaresque. What defeated him was war. It destroyed the mood out of which had come his best writing, it made the world of the Garoghlanians and Macauleys an impossible anachronism, and it so assaulted his faith in man that it left him without the resilience of mind to adjust his assumptions or accommodate his art.

With his separation from the service in September, 1945, came the inevitable self-assessment and the search for new directions. In February, 1943, he had married Carol Marcus, the daughter of a vice-president of Bendix Corporation. An attractive debutante who had taken a small part in *Across the Board on Tomorrow Morning,* she had joined Saroyan in Ohio, where he was stationed with the Signal Corps, and they had been married by a justice of the peace. Saroyan's London diary of 1944 records their faithful exchange of letters and other signs of mutual devotion. *Dear Baby,* which Saroyan prepared for the press in the summer of 1944, was dedicated to Carol: "What's said in this small book is not what I would finally say to you, but let it be the first of many gifts of love: a valentine made out of everything I was in the years long gone, before I saw you." Though determined in part by the kind of book they dedicate, these words are significant in pointing up Saroyan's instinct for seeing himself in terms of the past and his abiding need, only hinted at here, for guarding the continuity of this past-oriented self by assimilating to it all things new, even his love and marriage.

It is this self-absorption, as apparent in his life as in his art, that accounts for much of his difficulty in adjusting to the changing world; and it accounts, too, for the emotional tone of the fiction that was to rise out of the break-up of his marriage. In 1948 he brought his wife and two children—a son named Aram after Saroyan's grandfather and a daughter named Lucy after his grandmother—to New York, where he leased a large home near Oyster Bay, Long Island. But it soon became apparent that the marriage was in difficulty, and they stayed in their new home for only six months. Something of the anguish and uncertainty involved in the dissolution of the marriage can be drawn from its on-again-off-again nature: in the summer of 1948 a divorce action was dropped on the day of the scheduled hearing; in November, 1949, a divorce was obtained; in the spring of 1951 the couple remarried, only to have the second marriage end in divorce in 1952.[1]

The break-up of Saroyan's marriage constitutes the condition, the tone, the tension, and the particular urgency of much of his post-war writing, especially up through *The Laughing Matter*. It is not in any specific sense the *subject* of this writing, however. These stories of estrangement embrace the experience of many men. If it is true, as Saroyan has often said, that he is all of his characters, it is also true that no single character can be identified with him.[2] Whatever truth about the so-called *real* self that Saroyan projects into his fiction is there as an adjustment to the needs of the story. There are any number of versions of this self, and each is intended to portray something representative, not unique. What is sometimes called "the second self," the self that is implicit in the work, is never the same as the man writing the story, even when the personal equation seems close, as it often does in Saroyan.[3] As I commented earlier, criticism offered little help to him with respect to this distinction. Not clearly understanding it in his early period, he squandered some of his finest material through unnecessary and ineffectual attempts to disguise the presence of this "second self." In the face of much adverse criticism, however, he had the instinct to continue writing out of the materials of his own experience; and, by virtue of a prodigious amount of work, he finally learned to draw literary truth from autobiographical fact. He liked to use the word "allegorical" for this function, and in doing so he saw himself in the age-old storytelling tradition of Asia Minor. By the same token, when he quit trying to live the part of his characters, he made it much easier for his readers, undistracted by his own antics, to appreciate his fiction.[4]

II *Three Autobiographies*

We are now far enough away from his early work to realize that its durability depends in a very real way upon the reader's ability to see the "I" of the story apart from the identity of the author. A further indication of this essential difference lies in the obvious superiority of his short stories and novels to his autobiographies. Paradoxically, Saroyan has not been successful in straight autobiography. When making fiction of his life, he could be truly original, but his autobiographies are surprisingly conventional and lacking in distinction. They possess the cliché tone of rueful pleasure in recalling the joys of boyhood; the equally cliché profession of indifference to success; and, in respect to family, the ambivalent affection and resentment that one often finds in books of reminiscence. There is also the not quite suppressed note of impatience, at times of condescension, toward acquaintances and not-so-distant relatives. But the primary danger of autobiography for Saroyan is that it provides no curb for his sermonizing proclivities. The talk is discursive, unsorted, copious; it is flagrantly intrusive in his first autobiography, *The Bicycle Rider in Beverly Hills* (1952), more so in *Here Comes / There Goes / You Know Who* (1961), and nearly intolerable in *Not Dying* (1963).

The first of these is the best, not only because it relates to his boyhood but also because it utilizes an effective scheme of organization: riding a bike with his son is a good means of stimulating memory, gaining perspective, and arousing latent enthusiasms. The book has the merit of giving us the man, his attractive breeziness as well as his troublesome fondness for pseudo-philosophy. We see the young boy hawking newspapers in Fresno, drinking his fill of buttermilk for five cents, sneaking into movies, working for the telegraph office, pestering teachers at the Emerson School, and dropping out of high school without a diploma. And the book helps us understand better why estrangement has been prominent in his writing, for it speaks of the immigrant passage still fresh in the family memory (William was the only one of the four children who was born in the United States), the boy's awareness of belonging to an unpopular minority (five thousand Armenians in a town of twenty-five thousand), the death of his father, and the four years in the Fred Finch Orphanage in Oakland.

His other two book-length autobiographical essays have very little to commend them. They are distressing, indeed, to those who have followed Saroyan's career over the years and have excused his ungoverned volubility because it flowed from an irrepressible impulse to communicate. His writing continues with undiminished abundance, but its purpose now, as he candidly announces, is to earn as much money as possible. These two autobiographies are addressed to nothing more personal than his typewriter, from which he insists upon drawing a large daily quota of words. In 1958 he closed his home at Malibu Beach, California, where he had lived for six years, and went to Europe in hopes of earning enough money to pay his large tax debt. After living in Paris for about four years, he commented on the American expatriates of the 1920's, especially on Hemingway and Fitzgerald: "I feel part of them, but I *know* I am *not* a part of them. . . . There was something especially American about it. My San Francisco deal was rather Armenian, or at least European."[5] We see clearly that his move to Europe also reflected the ever-present dichotomy of this Armenian-American who never fully belonged to the American scene, except in one of its transitory phases. Actually, Saroyan's America had become almost pure solipsism, and a rapidly changing post-war America could find little of its contemporary self mirrored in his private world.

III *Four Recent Novels*

There is no better indication of the limiting effects of this growing solipsism than his most recent novel, *One Day in the Afternoon of the World.* In style it is as good as anything he has written: it is swift and lean, well-visualized, well-unified, and freer of reflective digressions than any other novel since *The Laughing Matter.* Yet it fails to reflect anything more representative than Saroyan's own weariness and disenchantment: "There comes a day in the afternoon of the world when a man simply wants to lie down and close his eyes."[6] Here the Saroyan protagonist is a tired, memory-haunted man who at the close of the book slips into a melancholy that is no broader than a nostalgia for his own particular past. It is an involvement with self that spoils his chances of deriving solace or lasting pleasure from the young lives he briefly touches in the story. Because the author gives us no indication that his vision is larger than that of his protagonist, the final effect of the novel is restricting and oppressive.

One Day in the Afternoon of the World is one of the four novels that he has published since 1953. The best of these is *Mama I Love You* (1956), "a fairy story in modern dress," as one reviewer described it.[7] Dedicated to his daughter, the story is told by nine-year-old Twink, an imaginative, fun-loving girl through whose eyes we see Mama Girl, a pert, charming woman intent upon making good in the theater. As in Saroyan's earlier books, there is no adult-child conflict; for the two are remarkably well tuned to each other and their conversations are lively and engaging. Though the novel is awkward and unconvincing when it tries to indicate some of the deeper aspects of adult restlessness, it handles the fundamentals of storytelling competently as it takes the mother and daughter through the excitement and terror of an entire production from the first readings, through casting, adjustments in script, tryouts in Philadelphia and Boston, and finally to opening night at the Belasco. The play is a hit, for Twink is after all a good fairy. The book was favorably received, on the whole. One reviewer felt that it deserves to be measured against the early plays and short stories.[8] Such a measurement, however, indicates the relative lightness of this later work.

The following year Saroyan published a companion piece, *Papa You're Crazy*, which he dedicated to his son. Though listed as a novel, it is autobiography presented in the form of an extended dialogue between father and son, with the latter as narrator. In effect, however, the boy is little more than a straight man for the adult; and the book is much less about a father-son relationship than about a writer who is growing desperate because of lack of money and loss of inspiration. Only rarely does

Saroyan's talent for vignette relieve an otherwise monotonous book. On the other hand, a father-daughter relationship comes through well, though briefly, in *One Day in the Afternoon of the World.* In its finest scene, the father takes his ten-year-old daughter for a walk on Fifth Avenue. It is "one of the most beautiful days of the year," he says; and the reader soon agrees, for the writing is alive with the spirit of mid-town New York in early fall, with the excitement of a World Series in the air.[9]

Boys and Girls Together (1963) is the least attractive, and one should note, the least characteristic, of these four recent novels. Though it achieves mastery of the low-keyed conversational exchange, its characters seem unable to determine the style of their own talk. They are too obviously props for his story. In tone, it resembles the literature of the absurd, for its people badly need what seems not to exist: love and understanding. It is the only book of Saroyan's in which the characters are predominantly callow, self-indulgent, and preoccupied with sex and drinking.

What often defeats Saroyan in his novels is lack of interest in character for its own sake. In his latest autobiographical interlude, *Not Dying,* a friend, in speaking of an earlier meeting with Saroyan, observes: "You weren't exactly rude, although the way you have makes most people hate you, if the word isn't too strong, a way of not really noticing anybody about you, not permitting them to become real to you, even, as if they were no more than figures in somebody's sleep, and not necessarily your own, as I am sure you are aware, and have always been." To which Saroyan replies: "Not always, but ten years ago word came to me in a roundabout way, and, ever since, I have been at work trying to correct this unfortunate condition, but I haven't made it, I haven't corrected it, I can't excuse it, I can't find an explanation for it, I know I do nothing rude deliberately."[10] This passage describes a characteristic of Saroyan's which is his, just like the shape of his chin or the color of his eyes; and, however it may complicate his relationship with people, it is, I am sure, his biggest handicap as a novelist. His best fiction in its longer forms is the witty *jeu d'esprit,* such as *Tracy's Tiger* or *Mama I Love You.*

IV *Return to the Short Story*: The Whole Voyald

His proper métier is the short story. His is an art of situation rather than action, of characters seen instantaneously, as it were, with their full quota of characteristics present from the beginning. They must be called "flat" in E. M. Forster's sense of this word, for they rarely surprise one. Yet they spring from an imagination so confident of their reality that we unconsciously assume their completeness; we are sure that Saroyan knows much more about them than he is obliged to tell. It is not surprising, therefore, that his best post-war book, despite its gauche title, *The Whole Voyald*, is a collection of short stories. Published in 1956, it is the first since *Dear Baby* (1944) to be made up entirely of short pieces. (*The Assyrian and Other Stories*, 1950, features the novelette.) "Voyald," Saroyan explains in his dedication, is not dialect but a way of saying void, voyage, and world at the same time. What distinguishes this writing from his pre-war fiction is the disenchantment that has come with wider knowledge. The mood is pervasive and imparts a strong unity to the collection, but it also has a curious effect of contracting the horizons. In place of the elegiac note, suggesting the sadness of uprooted people everywhere, that runs through such pieces as "Seventy Thousand Assyrians" and "The Poor and Burning Arab," *The Whole Voyald* gives us one man's melancholy.

Yet the technique is masterful, especially in the selection of detail and the blending of setting, character, and idea. The passing years have given Saroyan a greater concern for the idea, and thus these stories have a more pronounced heightening of effect than we find in his pre-war fiction. But they are also less spontaneous and sometimes too apparent in their symbolic intention. The effect he most characteristically seeks to achieve is illustrated by "The Play That Got Away." The narrator is an author who recalls an incident from his youth in the *Fiore d'Italia,* San Francisco: "At closing time one Saturday night I came upon a big Negro woman [who was] poking about in the enormous garbage can into which spoiled vegetables were being tossed. I went to the woman with an enormous cabbage to present to her. 'God bless you, son, no thanks,' she said. 'I'm just looking for a little spinach.'"[11] The speaker concludes: "The theatre is everywhere and the play was everywhere, but I was an unproven writer at the time, and so the play got away."

V *Saroyan and the Oral Tradition*

It is sparseness of detail and richness of implication toward which Saroyan directed his technique. The discipline of such art is consciously concealed by repetition of words and by other devices that suggest the casual directness of the spoken word. It is the quality of the fable, an art form which Saroyan had known from early boyhood. Indeed, the twin-fountains of his art are the storytelling tradition that is deep in his family history and the warm-hearted responsiveness to life characteristic of him. The most specific acknowledgment of the former influence appears in his Preface to the play *Sam Ego's House*:[12]

> Everything I write, everything I have ever written, is allegorical. This came to pass inevitably. One does not choose to write allegorically any more than one chooses to grow black hair on his head. The stories of Armenia, Kurdistan, Georgia, Persia, Syria, Arabia, Turkey and Israel are all allegorical, and apart from the fact that I heard these stories as a child told to me by both grandmothers, by great-aunts and great-uncles, and by friends of the family, I myself am a product of Asia Minor, hence the allegorical and the real are closely related in my mind.
>
> In fact all reality to me is allegorical, and I cannot so much as hear a commonplace American joke and not know and enjoy its deeper humor and meaning.

Long after the printing of books had become common in Asia Minor and the profession of writing well established, he adds, this tradition continued to be largely oral. Only in terms of this background can we understand Saroyan's incredibly large output: to him, the writer is a spinner of yarns—"You can tell a story a day if you just do it," he has recently been quoted as saying.[13] And interviewers frequently hear of countless pages of unpublished manuscript material which he has on hand.

This family tradition also makes more meaningful his reaction to Eric Bentley's criticism that he is a careless writer: "One cannot expect an Armenian to be an Englishman,"[14] a remark that is not inappropriate in view of our predominantly Anglo-Saxon critical tradition. But Saroyan is willing to admit the charge of carelessness, as he is the charge of sentimentality. In respect to the latter, he once commented that it is a very sentimental thing to be a human being. To the many criticisms of his underlying optimism, he has replied: "Out of ignorance and desperation, poverty and pain, for instance, emerges intelligence and grace, humor and resignation, decency and integrity. . . . I don't know why or how, precisely, this sort of thing happens, but I do know that it does happen and that I feel it is right for it to happen, although I know I am seldom equal to the job of making it seem *unquestionably* right—which is a matter of skill."[15]

Saroyan has worked hard to develop this skill. Though he has learned much from others, as I have pointed out, he has never consistently modeled his writing on other writers, nor has he ever been systematic in his reading. Yet the number of authors whom he mentions in his prefaces and autobiographical essays is surprisingly large; and there are anecdotes which reveal his interest in the personalities, if not in the writing, of people like James Joyce, George Bernard Shaw, and Gertrude Stein, with whom he exchanged letters and whom he met in San Francisco when she was motoring through the United States with Alice Toklas.[16] One of the few times he ever compared himself to another writer, he said: "Sean O'Casey has everything—humor, wisdom, characterization—and that underlying sense of tragedy which is painful comedy. His stuff . . . has truth and purpose. I can write a play like *Love's Old Sweet Song* that's just fun, but there's not much purpose to it. O'Casey can mix purpose with fun. I can't, and people heckle me for it."[17] In general, however, Saroyan's remarks on writers, especially those in his autobiographical essays, are notable for their lack of specific content and for the tendency to single out those who have had the least impact upon his own work.

Movies, vaudeville, and music, especially popular music, have been of great importance to his writing. Throughout his entire career he has drawn upon music for some of his most characteristic effects. He wrote the lyrics and tunes for several songs that were sung by Walter Huston in *Love's Old Sweet Song,* a play which he described as an extended song. For his most recently produced play, *Sam the Highest Jumper of Them All,* which was conceived as a song, he wrote the lyrics and tunes for four songs. His most successful venture into musical composition came in 1939 when he and his cousin, Ross Bagdasarian, wrote the words and music to "Come On-a My House." In 1951, when it was recorded by Rosemary Clooney for Columbia, it sold three-quarters of a million records in the first four weeks and soon appeared in fifteen different recordings, including Spanish and Armenian versions. At the time, Saroyan remarked to an interviewer from the *New Yorker* that songs came naturally to him: "Everything I've done has been a sort of song . . . The first story I wrote, 'The Daring Young Man on the Flying Trapeze,' was taken from a song."[18] In his plays that call for music other than that of his own composition, it is his custom to specify the particular selections. In *Across the Board on Tomorrow Morning,* for example, he called for the Gabriel Fauré "Impromptu for Harp."

"Come On-a My House," like many of Saroyan's songs, was adapted from Armenian folk music. Indeed, a great part of his writing—especially his fantasies for the stage and some of the best of his short stories—rest on imaginative and emotional patterns that are characteristic of folk art. Though Saroyan has been unswervingly self-centered in his writing, he has produced an art that is not, until recently at least, private in its images and implications. From the beginning it has evoked an extraordinarily large popular response, and the passing years have indicated its power to hold readers in large and faithful numbers. In their closeness to folk traditions his characters reflect aspects of our national life that are too little represented in our literature. The uprootedness of the immigrant and his problems of assimilation constitute an essential part of the American experience. The Italians, Greeks, Jews, and Armenians born of Saroyan's imagination continue to dwell in the minds of his readers after many years. Not only has he "charmed" a public into existence, as Elizabeth Bowen has aptly observed,[19] but he has provided it with a correlative for some of its most representative emotions.

Moreover, a generation too young to have read Saroyan during the 1930's and early 1940's is now manifesting enthusiasm for his work. His style—clear, swift, intense, and apparently casual—has begun to enjoy the distinction of imitators among new writers. His books are continually on demand in the circulating libraries, and they are difficult to find in the used-book stores. *The Daring Young Man* and *My Name is Aram* are available in inexpensive reprint editions, and his short stories and plays are often anthologized. In London, Faber and Faber continues to publish most of his current things, such as *The Cave Dwellers, Sam the Highest Jumper of Them All,* and *Settled out of Court,* the latter two neither performed nor published in this country; and it has recently reissued such earlier books as *The Daring Young Man, The Human Comedy, The Whole Voyald,* and *Tracy's Tiger.*

American literature has been written perhaps too exclusively from the point of view of its Anglo-Saxon origins. Indeed, a fundamental problem for Saroyan is that his inherited attitudes and tastes have placed him outside the mainstream of American culture. Because of his emphasis on the "good guys," or at least on the "happy guys," he has seemingly sinned against the high seriousness and pessimism of our literature. Instead of a literature of denial or of anger, his is one of affirmation: "In the time of your life, live." He has steadfastly refused to accept the prevailing ideals of composition and the predominant pessimism of Naturalism. Because his treatment of serious themes has often appeared casual, deeper implications have sometimes been overlooked. On the whole, however, the drama critics have been remarkably generous though Saroyan has always thought himself mistreated by them. Rarely has his fiction received careful consideration beyond the initial reviews. The occasional references one finds in scholarly journals often imply a note of regret that his extraordinary gifts have not been more fully developed.[20] At present, it seems clear that Saroyan's claim to an enduring reputation must rest on his pre-war writing, on the three or four plays that are as fresh and meaningful now as when they first appeared, and on the best of his short stories.

Notes and References

Chapter One

1. *Story,* IV (April, 1934), 2.
2. *Story,* IV (May, 1934), 2. See also the June issue (p. 95) and the October issue (p. 98) for indications of the enthusiasm for this new writer. "Resurrection of a Life," reprinted in Saroyan's second book, appeared in the November issue, 1934.
3. Saroyan dedicated his first book to Whit Burnett and Martha Foley.
4. *The Daring Young Man on the Flying Trapeze* (New York, 1934), pp. 9-13.
5. *Ibid.,* pp. 17-25.
6. *Ibid.* See pp. 133 and 137 for some of the more obvious imitations of Hemingway.
7. *Ibid.,* pp. 165-77. For other characters mentioned in this paragraph, see pp. 225-34, 43-50.
8. *Ibid.,* pp. 251-64.
9. *Ibid.,* pp. 27-41.
10. New York *Herald Tribune* (October 21, 1934), p. 9; (September 23, 1934), p. 3.
11. *New Republic,* CIII (November 18, 1940), 697-98; published also as *The Boys in the Back Room, Notes on California Novelists,* (San Francisco, 1941); reprinted in *Classics and Commercials* (New York, 1950).
12. *Hound and Horn,* VII (April: May, 1934). See also, Ray West, Jr., *The Short Story in America* (Chicago, 1952), pp. 22-23, 83. Mr. West observed that criticism could no longer take Saroyan's work seriously because it could no longer regard him "as a promising, if pretentious, young writer."
13. *New Yorker,* XII (February 22, 1936), 79-81.
14. New York *Herald Tribune* (February 23, 1936), p. 7. Though reviewing Saroyan's second book, Mr. Gregory was looking back to 1934.
15. *Saturday Review of Literature,* XI (October 20, 1934), 217, 221.
16. The quotation is from Irving Howe, *Sherwood Anderson* (New York, 1951), 246.
17. Edmund Wilson, *Axel's Castle* (New York, 1931), p. 292.

Chapter Two

1. *Esquire,* IV (August, 1935), 12; *Scribner's,* CI (April, 1936), 256; *New Yorker,* XII (February 22, 1936), 79-81; *Saturday Review of Literature,* XIII (February 22, 1936), 11.
2. New York *Herald Tribune* (February 23, 1936), p. 7; *The Nation,* CXLII (March 23, 1936), 387.

3. *New Republic,* LXXXVI (March 18, 1936), 172-73.
4. New York *Times* (February 23, 1936), p. 4.
5. *New Yorker,* XII (February 22, 1936), 79-81.
6. *Inhale and Exhale* (New York, 1936), pp. 437-38.
7. *Ibid.,* pp. 293-96, 396.
8. New York *Times* (February 23, 1936), pp. 4, 13.
9. *Inhale and Exhale,* pp. 87-93.
10. New York *Times* (February 23, 1936), pp. 4, 13.
11. The following sequence of six stories are of course scattered among the seventy-one items of *Inhale and Exhale,* and I bring them together here for the purpose of pointing to Saroyan's growth in independence as a writer. See pp. 222-29, 349-56, 93-100, 67-73, 363-70, 233-39.
12. Lionel Trilling has observed of Anderson that affirmations such as love and passion have the paradoxical effect of negating life, leaving it empty of meaning. *The Liberal Imagination* (New York, 1950), pp. 33-43.
13. *Three Times Three* (Los Angeles, 1936), pp. vii-xii.
14. Quoted by Richard Hoggart, *Auden, An Introductory Essay* (London, 1951), p. 17.
15. For references in this paragraph, see *Three Times Three,* pp. 99-100.
16. *Ibid.,* pp. 3-6.
17. Reviewing *Three Times Three,* William Troy noted that Saroyan should have overheard Gertrude Stein telling Hemingway that remarks are not literature. But Mr. Troy acknowledged too that Saroyan possessed "an abundance of feeling" and that the book showed unmistakable signs that he was beginning to recognize the need for "objective equivalents" of his feelings. *The Nation,* CXLIV (January 16, 1937), 77.
18. *Love, Here is My Hat and Other Short Romances* (New York, 1938), pp. 113, 112.
19. *Ibid.,* p. 114.
20. *Ibid.,* p. 121.
21. *The Trouble with Tigers* (New York, 1938), pp. 213-21.
22. *Ibid.,* pp. 86-89.
23. *Ibid.,* pp. 77-78.
24. *Ibid.,* p. 183.
25. *Ibid.,* p. 205.
26. *The Spectator,* CLXI (September 9, 1938), 413-14.
27. *Peace, It's Wonderful* (New York, 1939), p. 75.
28. *Ibid.* The stories referred to in this paragraph: "The War in Spain"; "A Number of the Poor"; "Piano"; "The Best and Worst People and Things of 1938"; "Johnny the Dreamer, Mary the Model at Magnin's, and Plato the Democrat."
29. *Ibid.,* p. 134.

Chapter Three

1. *Overland Monthly and Out West Magazine,* LXXXVI (December, 1928), 421, 424.
2. *The Daring Young Man on the Flying Trapeze,* pp. 59-63. The

entire sketch is redolent of Walt Whitman's assertion: "This is no book, Camerado, this is a man."

3. *Ibid.*, p. 267.

4. In addition to the stories mentioned in the paragraph above, see "Sleep in Heavenly Peace," in *The Daring Young Man,* and "My Picture in the Paper," in *Inhale and Exhale.*

5. *Inhale and Exhale,* p. 13.

6. *Ibid.*, pp. 257-65.

7. *Three Times Three,* pp. 11-23. For a fuller treatment of this valuable story, see Chapter Four.

8. *Ibid.*, p. 99.

9. *Ibid.*, pp. 41-51.

10. *Ibid.*, p. 62.

11. *Ibid.*, p. 135.

12. *New Republic,* XCII (August 25, 1937), 81.

13. New York *Times* (August 15, 1937), p. 6.

14. London *Times Literary Supplement* (October 23, 1937), p. 779.

15. *Little Children* (New York, 1937), pp. 3-12.

16. Saroyan made effective use of the pin-ball machine in *The Time of Your Life.*

17. *The Trouble with Tigers,* pp. 111-18.

18. *Peace, It's Wonderful,* pp. 53, 62.

19. *My Name is Aram* (New York, 1940), pp. vii-x.

20. Albert E. Stone, Jr., *The Innocent Eye* (New Haven, 1961) gives an excellent treatment of childhood in American literature.

21. *My Name is Aram,* pp. 31, 32.

22. *Ibid.*, pp. 99-101.

Chapter Four

1. In its final form, the play had no division into acts and scenes. The performance ran without interruption for one hour and a half.

2. Among the detractors were Wolcott Gibbs, Burns Mantle, and Sidney Whipple. The text of the play and many reviews, both favorable and unfavorable, are reprinted in Saroyan, *Three Plays* (New York, 1940).

3. Obey's *Noé* was translated into English in 1934 and published by Samuel French, New York. It was performed in 1935 at the Longacre Theatre, New York. See also John Gassner, *Theatre in Our Times* (New York, 1954), p. 212.

4. The texts of the plays are reprinted in *Three Plays.* Mary McCarthy, writing in *The Partisan Review,* spoke of the element of vaudeville in Saroyan's first two successful plays. See *Sights and Spectacles: Theatre Chronicles, 1937-1956* (New York, 1956), pp. 46-52. Philip Rahv also noted this similarity in the *American Mercury* (September, 1943).

5. The part of Joe was played by Eddie Dowling, who also directed and produced the play in conjunction with the Guild Theatre. He bought the script "sight-unseen" on the basis of his enthusiasm for *My Heart's*

in the Highlands. It opened at the Booth Theatre, New York, on Wednesday, October 25, 1939 and closed on April 6, 1940, after 185 performances.

6. Its popularity is attested to by a highly successful road tour; a successful revival at the New York City Center in 1955 with Franchot Tone, Lenka Peterson, Myron McCormack, Harold Lang, and John Carradine; a television production, "Playhouse 90" (October 9, 1958), which won wide acclaim for the play and for Jackie Gleason as Joe. I have had the pleasure of seeing the play produced in Spanish by students at the University of Saragossa, Spain; and performed again at Murcia, Spain, in a national drama contest (1958-59).

7. The phrase is Harold Clurman's, a strong admirer of this play. *Lies Like Truth* (New York, 1958), p. 220.

8. Reviewers did not single out this incident for special note, though Wolcott Gibbs asked mischievously if such tactics may not be a bit severe for the aging actor. *New Yorker,* XVI (May 11, 1940), 28.

9. Saroyan thus adds immeasurably to the satirical implications of the incident; but the climactic decision of the play is made offstage, which indicates how little interest the author had in plot.

10. Eddie Dowling received a great deal of praise for his direction, as did Walter Huston and Jessie Royce Landis for their performances.

11. The meeting is reported in the New York *Times* (May 4, 1940), p. 12. As a reminder of the prevailing mood of the time, I note that the runner-up for the prize was Robert Sherwood's *There Shall Be No Night.*

12. The announcement of the Prize and the exchange of telegrams related to it are published in the New York *Times* (May 7, 8, 1940), pp. 1, 25. Other Pulitzer Prize awards that year went to John Steinbeck for *The Grapes of Wrath,* Carl Sandburg for his biography of Lincoln, and Mark Van Doren for his *Collected Poems.*

13. *Razzle Dazzle* (New York, 1942), p. 179.

14. Act II, scene ii.

15. Saroyan, *Three Plays* (New York, 1941), pp. 3-5.

16. *New Republic,* CIV (May 5, 1941), 632-33.

17. *The Nation,* CLII (May 3, 1941), 537-38.

18. *New Yorker,* XVII (May 3, 1941), 30.

19. *New Republic,* CIV (May 12, 1941), 664.

20. See, for example, New York *Times* (March 21, 1942), p. 13. *Across the Board on Tomorrow Morning* had its first production in California, playing for two weeks in February, 1941, at the Pasadena Playhouse. Saroyan was disappointed in the response. Never one to be intimidated by custom, he arranged with Gilmore Brown, the supervising director, to have the play performed twice in succession at each performance, so that those who cared to see it twice could do so. There were five such performances. Saroyan insisted that the play was good, not because he wrote it, but because it was "simultaneously sad and funny, which is also the way of reality." *Three Plays* (1941), pp. 213-15.

21. New York *Times* (August 18, 1942), p. 17. For a defense of Saroyan's work as director see Stark Young, *New Republic,* CVII (October

12, 1942), 466, an article which also indicates the most commonly accepted criticisms of Saroyan's direction.

22. *The American Mercury,* LV (November, 1942), 573-75.

23. The play is published in *Three Plays* (1941).

24. *The Nation,* CXCIII (December 2, 1961), 460.

25. The play is reprinted in *Razzle Dazzle,* p. 428.

26. The description is Arthur Gelb's, who also noticed the grim timeliness of the setting. New York *Times* (October 23, 1961), p. 22.

27. *Razzle Dazzle,* p. 367. The play is also reprinted in *The Best One-Act Plays of 1941,* edited by Margaret Mayorga (New York, 1941), pp. 211-31.

28. *New Yorker,* XVIII (October 10, 1942), 30; New York *Times,* (September 30, 1942), p. 28. *Hello Out There* was composed in the summer of 1941 and produced in California at the Lobero Theatre in Santa Barbara, September, 1941, as a curtain raiser to George Bernard Shaw's *The Devil's Disciple.* In New York it formed a double bill at the Belasco with G. K. Chesterton's *Magic.*

29. These plays have been published individually by Samuel French, New York, and in collection by Harcourt, Brace, New York, and Faber and Faber, London.

30. *The Nation,* CLXXX (April 30, 1955), 364-66.

31. First published as *Jim Dandy: A Play* (Cleveland, 1941), and revised as *Jim Dandy: Fat Man in a Famine* (New York, 1947). See the stage directions to Act I of the later edition for the source of this quotation.

32. *The Cave Dwellers* (New York, 1958), p. 105. Saroyan did not like the production, nor did Wolcott Gibbs of the *New Yorker* or Patrick Dennis of the *New Republic.* Walter Kerr, whose final verdict was also negative, located its failure not in Saroyan's irreverence for form but in his "pretentious and intrusive language." These reviews, and others, are reprinted in *The Cave Dwellers,* pp. 159-61, 175-77, 137-39, 151-54. In general, however, critics were once again eager for a Saroyan play to succeed. The majority chose to concentrate on its beauty and to overlook its deficiencies. Though not a hit by Broadway standards, it ran from October 19, 1957, to January 11, 1958, closing after ninety-eight performances.

Chapter Five

1. Though Saroyan was often eager to work in pictures, his motives were not those of profit. In 1946 he sold the screen rights for *The Time of Your Life* to the Cagney brothers, refusing larger offers from Warner Brothers and Metro-Goldwyn-Mayer because he felt James Cagney should play the lead. These two incidents can be followed in the New York *Times*: (December 21, 1941), pp. ix, 5; (May 5 1942), p. 17; (May 10, 1942), pp. viii, 3; (November 25, 1943), p. 40; (December 15, 1946), pp. ii, 5. See also *New Yorker,* XVIII (July 11, 1942), 10. For another expression of his angry reaction to the MGM experience, see my discussion of *Get Away Old Man* on p. 119.

2. *The Adventures of Wesley Jackson* (New York, 1946), pp. 267, 278.

3. *Dear Baby* (New York, 1944), pp. 83-90. For background information on the nature and the antiquity of this religious thought I am indebted to Rudolph Otto, *The Idea of the Holy* (New York, 1958) and to Mircea Eliade, *The Sacred and the Profane* (New York, 1959) and *Patterns in Comparative Religion* (New York, 1958). For the spirit of the Eastern religious thought of which Armenian Christianity is part, see Timothy Ware, *The Orthodox Church* (New York and London, 1963).

4. *Dear Baby,* pp. 75-78.

5. *The Assyrian and Other Stories* (New York, 1950). For "The Writer on Writing," see pp. xiii-xxxix; for *The Assyrian,* pp. 1-89; for "The Cocktail Party," pp. 239-68. *The Poet at Home,* pp. 131-85, another novella, gives a happier picture of an author's private life.

6. *Ibid.,* p. 251.

7. *Ibid.,* p. xviii.

8. *Ibid.,* pp. xxiv, xxv, xviii.

9. *Ibid.,* p. xx.

10. *Ibid.,* p. 18.

11. The quotation is from Saroyan's preface to *Sam Ego's House,* which preface was written in 1949, the same year as the preface to *The Assyrian.* It is published in *Don't Go Away Mad and Other Plays* (New York. 1949), also in London by Faber and Faber. See also Nona Balakian, "So Many Saroyans," the only reviewer who, so far as I know, has noted Saroyan's important self-discovery. *New Republic,* CXXIII (August 7, 1950), 19-20.

12. *Ibid.,* p. xx.

13. William Saroyan, "Americans in Paris, 1929," *New Republic,* CXLVIII (February 9, 1963), 26-28.

14. *The Assyrian and Other Stories,* p. xix.

15. *Rock Wagram* (Garden City, 1951), pp. 96, 114; for quotations above see pp. 109, 102.

16. C. J. Rollo in *The Atlantic Monthly,* CLXXXVII (April, 1951), 78.

17. New York *Times* (March 18, 1951), p. 5. See *Rock Wagram,* p. 103.

18. New York *Herald Tribune* (November 18, 1951), p. 19.

19. *Laughing Matter* (Garden City, 1953), pp. 73, 118, 120, 223.

20. John Brooks of the *New Yorker* staff, reviewing in the New York *Times* (March 8, 1953), VII, 5. Elizabeth Bowen's review appeared in the *New Republic,* CXXVIII (March 9, 1953), 18-19. See also New York *Herald Tribune* (March 22, 1953), p. 15. *Atlantic Monthly,* CXCI (May, 1953), 81; *Saturday Review of Literature,* XXXVI (March 7, 1953), 56.

Chapter Six

1. Saroyan's marriage and divorce can be traced in the New York *Times* under the following dates: (February 25, 1943), 23; (July, 15, 1948), 21; (November 17, 1949), 15; (March 22, 1951), 41; (October 5, 1951), 24; (January 6, 1952), 80; (January 27, 1952), 36; (March 7,

1952), 17. Also see Saroyan's article, "The Funny Business of Marriage," *Saturday Evening Post* (October 5, 1963), 44-45.

2. See for example, *One Day in the Afternoon of the World* (New York, 1964), p. 34; *Don't Go Away Mad* (New York, 1949), p. 17.

3. See Wayne C. Booth, *The Rhetoric of Fiction* (Chicago, 1961), for an excellent discussion of this distinction.

4. There are many amusing examples of these antics. He wrote to the editors of *The Nation*: "I would like to protest against the type of reviewer your magazine has been assigning to my books lately. The reviews seem to be brilliant but are invariably unfriendly and scornful. This is no way to treat a great writer, I believe. In the future I would appreciate it very much if you would allow personal friends of mine to review my books." *The Nation,* CXLIV (April 23, 1938), 487. Again in September he wrote: "I am editing 'An Anthology of Lousy Writing,' and want contributions from good published writers who have at one time written badly. Contributions must be worse than just ordinarily bad and their authors must be better than just ordinarily good. Each contributor is invited to comment on his contribution." *The Nation,* CXLVII (September 10, 1938), 252.

5. *New Republic,* CXLVIII (February 7, 1963), 26-28.

6. *One Day in the Afternoon of the World,* p. 28.

7. *Atlantic Monthly,* CXLVIII (July, 1956), 86.

8. New York *Times* (May 27, 1956), p. 4.

9. *One Day in the Afternoon of the World,* p. 149.

10. *Not Dying, An Autobiographical Interlude* (New York, 1963), p. 23.

11. *The Whole Voyald and Other Stories* (Boston, 1956), p. 93.

12. Reprinted in *Don't Go Away Mad and Other Plays.* See also *Saroyan's Fables* (New York, 1941), a small book which retells traditional fables.

13. "In and Out of Books," by Lewis Nichols, the New York *Times* (April 12, 1964).

14. *Don't Go Away Mad and Other Plays,* p. 24.

15. *Ibid.,* p. 25.

16. For the James Joyce reference, see *Three Plays* (1941), p. 105; for Bernard Shaw references, see *The Bicycle Rider in Beverly Hills,* pp. 126, 154, *Here Comes / There Goes / You Know Who,* pp. 8. 54, 241, 265; for Gertrude Stein, see "Some Thoughts About Gertrude Stein," *The Reporter,* IX (October 13, 1953), 39-40, a review of *The Flowers of Friendship: Letters Written to Gertrude Stein.* This book reprints Saroyan's letter dated November 15, 1934. See also: John Malcolm Brinnin, *The Third Rose: Gertrude Stein and Her World,* (Boston, 1959), pp. 341-42; Elizabeth Sprigge, *Gertrude Stein: Her Life and Work* (New York, 1957), p. 186.

17. "Private Saroyan and the War," by Ralph Allen, New York *Times Magazine* (June 4, 1944). p. 46.

18. *New Yorker,* XXVII (September 8, 1951), 31. Saroyan has also written such miscellaneous musical pieces as "An Italian Opera in English," "Notes for a Musical Review," a ballet scenario entitled "Bad Men in the West." He also wrote a ballet entitled "A Theme in the Life of the Great

American Goof." It was produced in New York at the Center Theatre by the Ballet Theatre, Inc. in January, 1940. These titles are all published in *Razzle Dazzle*.

19. *New Republic*, CXXVIII (March 9, 1953), 18-19.

20. See, for example, Edmund Wilson, *The Shores of Light, A Literary Chronicle of the Twenties and Thirties* (New York, 1952), pp. 605-6. Mark Shorer, "Technique as Discovery," reprinted in John Aldridge, *Critiques and Essays on Modern Fiction, 1920-1951* (New York, 1952), pp. 81-82; also reprinted in William Van O'Connor, *Forms in Modern Fiction* (Minneapolis, 1948); appeared originally in *Hudson Review*, I (Spring, 1948).

Selected Bibliography

PRIMARY SOURCES

Most of the fiction listed below appeared originally in periodicals; many of the titles, especially of his plays, have appeared in several editions in the United States and abroad. I am listing the principal American editions, those most readily available.

The Daring Young Man on the Flying Trapeze and Other Stories. New York: Random House, 1934.

Inhale and Exhale. New York: Random House, 1936.

Three Times Three. Los Angeles: The Conference Press, 1936.

Little Children. New York: Harcourt, Brace, 1937.

Love, Here is My Hat and Other Short Romances. New York: Modern Age Books, 1938.

The Trouble with Tigers. New York: Harcourt, Brace, 1938.

Peace, It's Wonderful. New York: Starling Press, 1939.

My Name is Aram. New York: Harcourt, Brace, 1940.

Three Plays. New York: Harcourt, Brace, 1940.

Three Plays. New York: Harcourt, Brace, 1941.

Saroyan's Fables. New York: Harcourt, Brace, 1941.

Razzle-Dazzle. New York: Harcourt, Brace, 1942.

The Human Comedy. New York: Harcourt, Brace, 1943.

Get Away Old Man. New York: Harcourt, Brace, 1944.

Dear Baby. New York: Harcourt, Brace, 1944.

The Adventures of Wesley Jackson. New York: Harcourt, Brace, 1946.

Jim Dandy: Fat Man in a Famine. New York: Harcourt, Brace, 1947.

The Saroyan Special. New York: Harcourt, Brace, 1948.

Don't Go Away Mad and Other Plays. New York: Harcourt, Brace, 1949.

Twin Adventures. New York: Harcourt, Brace, 1950.

The Assyrian and Other Stories. New York: Harcourt, Brace, 1950.

Rock Wagram. New York: Doubleday, 1951.

Tracy's Tiger. New York: Doubleday, 1951.

The Bicycle Rider in Beverly Hills. New York: Scribner's, 1952.

The Laughing Matter. New York: Doubleday, 1953.

The Whole Voyald and Other Stories. Boston: Little, Brown, 1956.

Mama I Love You. Boston: Little, Brown, 1956.

Papa You're Crazy. Boston: Little, Brown, 1957.

The Cave Dwellers. New York: Putnam, 1958.

William Saroyan Reader. New York: Braziller, 1958.

Here Comes / There Goes / You Know Who. New York: Simon and Schuster, 1961.

Boys and Girls Together. New York: Harcourt, Brace and World, 1963.
Not Dying. New York: Harcourt, Brace and World, 1963.
One Day in the Afternoon of the World. New York: Harcourt, Brace and World, 1964.
After Thirty Years: The Daring Young Man on the Flying Trapeze. New York: Harcourt, Brace and World, 1964.

SECONDARY SOURCES

Especially significant critical reactions are described in the text and notes. This list contains a selection of notable criticisms.

ATKINSON, BROOKS. *Broadway Scrapbook*. New York: Theatre Arts, 1947. See also New York *Times* (May 3, 1940), p. 16; (April 22, 1941), p. 17; (March 21, 1942), p. 13; (August 18, 1942), p. 17; (September 30, 1942), p. 28. Consistently favorable treatment of Saroyan's plays.

BALAKIAN, NONA. "So Many Saroyans," *New Republic*, CXXIII (August 7, 1950), 19-20. Very helpful comments on the allegorical in Saroyan's writing.

BOWEN, ELIZABETH. "In Spite of Words," *New Republic*. CXXVIII (March 9, 1953), 18-19. Describes Saroyan's service to the American short story.

BROWN, JOHN MASON. *Broadway in Review*. New York: W. W. Norton, 1940. Saroyan has contributed to the theater through his handling of mood and his "bifocal exposure in time."

BURGUM, EDWIN B. "The Lonesome Young Man on the Flying Trapeze," *Virginia Quarterly Review*, XX (Summer, 1944), 392-403. Reprinted as chapter fifteen of *The Novel and the World's Dilemma*, New York: Oxford University Press, 1947. Saroyan wrote because he needed to be accepted.

CANBY, HENRY SEIDEL. "Armenian Picaresque," *Saturday Review of Literature*, XXIII (December 28, 1940), 5. *My Name is Aram* is a genuine, significant contribution to American literature.

CARPENTER, FREDERIC I. "The Time of Saroyan's Life," *Pacific Spectator*, I (Winter, 1947), 88-96. Saroyan reaffirms the old American faith of Emerson and Whitman.

CLURMAN, HAROLD. *Lies Like Truth*. New York: Macmillan, 1958. *The Time of Your Life* is "a little classic" of the American theater. See also *The Nation*, CXCIII (December 2, 1961), 460.

FISHER, WILLIAM J. "What Ever Happened to Saroyan?" *College English*, XVI (March, 1955), 336-40. Saroyan helped to restore perspective to our literature, and by 1940 he had become a national legend; but he lost ground when he began to explain his optimism.

FLOAN, HOWARD R. "Saroyan and Cervantes' Knight," *Thought*, XXXIII (Spring, 1958), 81-92. Considers quixotic patterns in Saroyan's prewar writing.

GASSNER, JOHN. *The Theatre in Our Times.* New York: Crown Publishers, 1954. Saroyan helped arouse the Broadway playgoer out of his lethargy.

———. *Theatre at the Crossroads.* New York: Holt, 1960. Compares Saroyan with Truman Capote.

HATCHER, HARLAN. "William Saroyan," *English Journal,* XXVIII (March, 1939), 167-77. Concedes that there is some truth to the "half-genius, half-phony" charge made against Saroyan but singles out individual stories that reveal great poignancy and remarkable understanding.

KAZIN, ALFRED. New York *Herald Tribune* (August 15, 1937), p. 4. A review of *Little Children* which points up Saroyan's failings but at the same time suggests something of his especial qualities of imagination.

———. "The Cymbolon," *New Republic,* CVIII (March 1, 1943), 289-91. Praises *The Human Comedy* as a series of effectively written scenes but finds it deficient as a novel.

KRUTCH, JOSEPH WOOD. *The Nation,* CXLVIII (May 6, 1939), 538; CL (May 18, 1940), 635; CLII (May 3, 1941), 537-38; CLV (October 10, 1942), 357. Perceptive remarks on Saroyan's drama, emphasizing his Romanticism.

———. *The Literary History of the United States.* Ed. by Robert Spiller, Willard Thorp et. al. New York: Macmillan, 1946. Relates Saroyan to the American theater.

MCCARTHY, MARY. *Sights and Spectacles.* New York: Farrar, Straus and Cudahy, 1956. Emphasizes the authenticity and innocence of Saroyan.

NATHAN, GEORGE JEAN. *The Magic Mirror.* New York: Knopf, 1960. See also "First Nights and Passing Judgments," *Esquire,* XIII (February, 1940), 78, 117; "Saroyan: Whirling Dervish of Fresno," *American Mercury,* II (November, 1940), 303-8, and other articles in the same periodical for sympathetic but sharply critical discussions of Saroyan.

PEDEN, WILLIAM. *Saturday Review of Literature,* XXXIII (February 4, 1950), 15-16. Brief but helpful attempt to define Saroyan's contribution to the American short story.

RAHV, PHILIP. "Regular Guy," *The Nation,* CXLVI (March 26, 1938), 363-64. Sees a changing Saroyan.

———. "William Saroyan: A Minority Report," *American Mercury,* LVII (September, 1943), 371-77. Objects to Saroyan's tendency to state rather than to represent his themes.

REMENYI, JOSEPH. "William Saroyan: A Portrait," *College English,* VI (November, 1944), 92-100. The happiness Saroyan spreads prevents him from being a searcher for truth in the philosophic sense.

ROSENFELD, ISAAC. "On One Built for Two," *New Republic,* CXXVII (December 8, 1952), 27-28. An analytical description of Saroyan's writing.

SCHULBERG, BUDD. "Saroyan: Ease and Unease on the Flying Trapeze," *Esquire,* LIV (October, 1960), 85-91. Critical and biographical sketch reflecting personal associations with Saroyan.

STRAUMAN, HEINRICH. *American Literature in the Twentieth Century.*

London: Hutchinson's, 1951. Discusses Saroyan's work in its relationship to dream and reality.

TRILLING, DIANA. *The Nation,* CLIX (December 2, 1944), 697. A very brief but highly suggestive attempt to illustrate the best and the worst of Saroyan.

WILSON, EDMUND. *Classics and Commercials.* New York: Farrar, Straus, 1950; *The Shores of Light.* New York: Farrar, Straus and Young, 1952. An appreciation of Saroyan's uniqueness combined with concern for his lack of self-discipline.

YOUNG, STARK. *New Republic,* CII (June 3, 1940), 760; CIV (May 12, 1941), 664; CVII (August 31, 1942), 257; CVII (October 12, 1942), 466. Finely discerning remarks on Saroyan's imagination and on his work as director.

Index

Index